New Zealand Sporting Disasters, Disappointments & Curiosities

RIP
"ALL BLACK DAYS"
·1949·
PLAYED 6 TESTS
LOST 6 TESTS

New Zealand Sporting Disasters, Disappointments & Curiosities

Keith Quinn

Cartoons by George Martin

RANDOM
HOUSE
NEW ZEALAND LTD

Random House New Zealand Ltd
(An imprint of the Random House Group)

18 Poland Road
Glenfield
Auckland 10
NEW ZEALAND

Associated companies, branches and
representatives throughout the world.

First published 1986
Reprinted 1986
This edition 1994
© Keith Quinn 1986, 1994
ISBN 1 86941 222 2
Printed in Hong Kong

Contents

Acknowledgements

In researching the stories for this book the author made reference to the following books:

The Encyclopedia of New Zealand Rugby, R. H. Chester and N. A. C. MacMillan (Moa Publications, 1981)

Men in Black, R. H. Chester and N. A. C. MacMillan (Moa Publications, 1988)

A Century of Rugby, A. R. Veysey (Organ Bros, 1969)

New Zealand Soccer — The Impossible Dream, Ian Walter and Ian Garner (Hodder & Stoughton, 1983)

The Games, Ron Palenski and Terry Maddaford (Moa Publications, 1983)

The Wisden Book of Test Cricket, Bill Frindall (MacDonald and Janes, 1979)

New Zealand International Cricket 1894–74, Arthur Carman (Sporting Publications, 1975)

New Zealand First-Class Cricket, Francis Payne

Australian Sporting Almanack, Jim Shepherd

A Noble Breed, Bill Mackie (Wilson & Horton, 1974)

Memorable Moments in New Zealand Sport, Don Cameron (ed.) (Moa Publications, 1979)

New Zealand's Champion Sportswomen, Dorothy Simons (Moa Publications: Dominion Breweries, 1982)

Haka! The All Blacks Story, Winston McCarthy (Pelham Books, 1968)

The author also referred extensively to the files of:

The New Zealand Rugby Almanack
The New Zealand Cricket Almanack
The New Zealand Herald
The Auckland Star
The Dominion
The Evening Post
The Press
The Otago Daily Times
The New Zealand Sportsman
Sport Digest.

The author would also like to thank the following people for invaluable assistance and support: Ray Richards, Anne Quinn, Raynor Wilson, Garry Ward, Bernie Wood, Christine Archer, Grahame Thorne, George Martin (for his many fine cartoons), and Peter Sellers. The following newspapers, photographers and publications are also to be thanked for contributing illustrations for this book:

The New *Zealand Newspapers Group*
New Zealand Herald
The Press
The Otago Daily Times
The New Zealand Netball Association
Ross Setford
Peter Bush

Preface

Over the years I have read hundreds of sports books, and I have often reflected on how many of them are concerned with champions and winning teams. Such a preoccupation is neither surprising nor undeserved, yet this compilation is intended to go some small way towards redressing the balance and reminding sports fans of the days of dreadful failure as well as those of success. It is, if you like, a celebration of the loser.

The book's original working title was, indeed, 'Disasters and Disappointments', but as it progressed I found myself coming across many bizarre and weird incidents and facts, so much so that I felt that they had to be included as well. Furthermore, there ran through my research — and there runs through this book — a rich vein of humour which proves that however seriously we take our sport, however much we like to win, we can (or many of us can) nevertheless look on the funny side of even the most abject defeat. If every cloud has a silver lining, then every sporting disaster has a humorous one.

KEITH QUINN

George Martin
Cartoonist for this book

George Martin was once called the 'Mr Versatile' of New Zealand sport. Not only is he a brilliant cartoonist and sports caricaturist but he can rightfully claim to have 'been there — done that' on the sports field.

As an eighteen-year-old George Martin won the New Zealand Pole Vault Championship in 1950 and competed in the Empire Games in Auckland that same year. Months later he played at centre three-quarter for the Wellington rugby team against the British Isles, marking such notables in midfield as Bleddyn Williams and Jack Matthews — both listed among the all-time greats of Welsh Rugby.

In 1951, seeking further experiences from the world of sport, George was in Australia where his football talents found him making his professional debut in the tough world of Sydney Rugby League. He played for the North Sydney Club and in 1952 was voted among the top five players of the year by the *Sydney Morning Herald*. He made the Rest of Australia team that played against the Kangaroos on their return from their international tour to Great Britain.

On returning to New Zealand, Martin turned his hand to local Rugby League and softball. He was a New Zealand Kiwi triallist in League and played softball for the Hutt Valley, North Island and New Zealand Black (against New Zealand White).

When he retired from more active participation in physical games Martin turned his hand to golf where his interest still lies today. He soon notched up club championship wins in the Junior, Intermediate and Senior grades at his home course of Shandon and for eight years held the course record there. George Martin these days still plays several rounds a week.

He is a colleague of author Keith Quinn and recently retired after a career as a graphic artist with Television New Zealand.

Introduction

A New Zealand cricket team is dismissed for 26 in a test match. An All Black team loses six tests out of six in a single year. These are but two of the lowest moments in New Zealand sport and they naturally receive space in this book. But defeat often conjures up the wryest of humour — an element that could not be excluded from a book like this.

This was the most disastrous sporting occasion in New Zealand's history, no doubt about it. Whether you were pro or anti the 1981 Springbok tour, scenes like this protest plane flying over Eden Park during third test made the whole thing a mess — whether you were playing or watching. *Photograph by Ross Setford*

However, the sporting disaster is not the prerogative of the famous international star. A disaster worth retelling can befall any person or team with the most modest of credentials. Like the Canterbury Club rugby team that a few years ago took its place on the field for the final match of the season with only fourteen men — the fifteenth was in a toilet cubicle under the grandstand wrestling with a jammed door! And how many social cricket teams have turned up for a match to find that no one has remembered to bring the bats or ball or pads, which are so essential to actually playing? Or the motor racing driver who accidentally put his car in reverse gear at a Le Mans-type race start to find himself and his car roaring off backwards down the circuit while everyone else in the race went in the opposite direction?

For the purposes of healthy argument I have made a list of what I think

were the ten greatest disasters of New Zealand sporting history. These are the events that I feel have had the greatest effect on New Zealand's sporting society as a whole. The effect was a mixture of consternation, upset, concern, anger and even despair felt by a large percentage of our population. My top ten are:

1 The 1981 and 1985 Springbok rugby tour controversies. (This will be the first and only mention of those tours in this book.) Whatever viewpoint one took of the rights and wrongs of the South African tour of New Zealand in 1981 or the proposed tour in 1985, they can hardly be rated anything but abject failures, in a public relations sense, for the game of rugby. The repercussions on New Zealand society in general as a result of those two seasons made the two tours the backdrop for some of the saddest days in New Zealand sports and social history.

2 The prevention of the bulk of New Zealand's team from attending the 1980 Olympic Games in Moscow. (To support an American boycott in order to protest against the Russian invasion of Afghanistan was a huge disappointment to New Zealand sportsmen. Many are the strong feelings that still exist towards the New Zealand Government of the day for withdrawing its support for a New Zealand team.)

3 Cancellation of the 1973 South African rugby tour of New Zealand by the then Prime Minister, Norman Kirk. (The huge rugby populace of New Zealand was greatly angered by what they felt was a change of mind by Mr Kirk over a very sensitive issue.)

Away from political matters, the true sporting disasters appear on the list:

4 The non-awarding of a try to Bob Deans of the All Black rugby team in the match New Zealand versus Wales in Cardiff in 1905. (To a young New Zealand nation the referee's decision, which robbed the All Blacks of an unbeaten tour record, had angry repercussions that have not truly disappeared even after eighty years.)

5 The sending home of All Black prop forward Keith Murdoch from the 1972–3 All Black tour of Great Britain, for disciplinary reasons. (Again, the big rugby populace wanted more reasons for his dismissal than were given at the time. Criticism of the All Blacks by thirteen British newspapers was viewed with considerable anger by outraged New Zealanders.)

6 The sending off of Colin Meads for alleged rough play in a rugby international in Edinburgh on the 1967 All Black tour. (Meads was a god to New Zealand rugby fans who could never see wrong in any of his actions on the field, especially when he was playing for his country. This was one of the biggest media stories of the day in New Zealand.) The dismissal of Cyril Brownlie from the England–New Zealand match in 1924–5 also caused much comment at the time.

7 The New Zealand cricket team being dismissed for 26 in an innings of a test cricket match against England at Auckland in 1955. (The word 'humiliation' is allied to 'disaster' here. All New Zealand was devastated that our cricketers could play so poorly. It was, and still is, the lowest score any country has made in a test match.)

8 The losing of six rugby tests in one season by the All Blacks in 1949. (Not only was the top New Zealand team humbled 4–0 by South Africa but a 'second' New Zealand squad, allowed to be called All Blacks, were also beaten two games to none, by Australia. A rugby nation, seeking pride in its national game in the first major season after the war, was desperately downcast at losing so often.)

9 The New Zealand rugby league team losing 4–3 to South Africa at Auckland in 1963. (At the time rugby league was a game New Zealand had a high world ranking in. The South African team, on its first and only overseas tour, had been hugely thrashed by Australia just days before. Conditions at Carlaw Park, muddy and cold, should have favoured the New Zealanders rather than the inexperienced South Africans.)

10 The New Zealand soccer team's world tour in 1964. In fifteen matches spread throughout eight countries the team won only once (and that only in the last tour match, against the San Francisco All-Stars!).

To me a 'diappointment' is a sporting 'disaster' that had a lesser degree of significance for the New Zealand sporting public. Disappointment tends to be of a more personal nature than the previously mentioned disasters you have just read about, and which were of national concern.

Here are my top ten New Zealand sporting disappointments:

1 New Zealand's collapse to 44 for the loss of 6 wickets in the final of the one-day cricket series with Australia in Melbourne in 1983. (The New Zealand public had great expectations of their team doing well against the old rivals, Australia. Only a later display of superb hitting by Lance Cairns, which improved the New Zealand team's final innings total, saved the day from being a huge cricketing disaster.)

2 The black day New Zealand's three major sporting codes suffered on 2 November 1985. On this day the New Zealand rugby and rugby league teams both had chances in faraway places to clinch important test series. On the

same day the New Zealand soccer team, also overseas, had a chance to consolidate their place as a real contender for making the 1986 World Cup soccer finals in Mexico.

The three internationals were to be played over a time span of thirteen hours and many Kiwi households made elaborate preparations in order to be free to watch the matches via TVNZ's live telecasts.

Sadly, the day (a Sunday in New Zealand) ended with none of the three teams earning a win. The best result was a 21–21 draw by the All Black rugby team in their second test match in Buenos Aires against the Pumas of Argentina. The Kiwi rugby league team lost 6–24 to Great Britain (after New Zealand had brilliantly won the first test) and the All White soccer team lost 0–2 to Australia, thus bowing out of contention for a finals place at Mexico.

The next morning all the sports pages of the morning's press carried subdued and sad stories reflecting a nation of sports fans who had all hoped that the Kiwi sportsmen, in their three important games, could have outshone their opponents.

3 The underarm bowling incident at Melbourne in the one-day cricket series of 1981 in which an already proven New Zealand sporting hero, Brian McKechnie, was prevented from attempting a six hit that would have beaten Australia. The Australian prevention came in the form of an underarm delivery by Australia's Trevor Chappell. (Watching the match live on television, New Zealanders were very scornful of the Australian tactic. Even the Prime Minister expressed a dis-

Another big disappointment for New Zealand sport: Sylvia Potts tumbles on the track at the Edinburgh Commonwealth Games of 1970. Officially she finished last in the 1500 metres event, after being inches from a gold medal.

pleasure that echoed the feelings of most Kiwi cricket fans.)

4 The breaking of an arm by Colin Meads on the All Blacks tour of South Africa in 1970. (Meads was still a god three years after being sent off in Scotland and his unavailability for the first half of the vital tour of South Africa because of his arm injury was a major disappointment to New Zealanders, who were hoping that the All Blacks would at last win a test rugby series against South Africa in their country.)

5 The untimely death of Ken Wadsworth in 1975, which robbed New Zealand cricket of a world-class wicket-keeper and test cricket competitor. (Wadsworth died of cancer aged 29. Had he lived, he would certainly have been an even longer-serving New Zealand player. Although keepers such as Warren Lees and Ian Smith emerged after his passing, Wadsworth was sorely missed in the New Zealand cricket scene.)

6 Scoring only 6 penalty goals against the British Isles in the first rugby test of 1959 at Dunedin. The disappointment was that the penalties helped New Zealand to a win even though the British Lions scored superb tries. (British rugby writers condemned New Zealand that day as being dull and stodgy footballers, totally reliant on the boot of the fullback Don Clarke.) The result was a win to New Zealand but in a hollow and therefore disappointing manner.

7 The failure of the New Zealand Commonwealth Games selectors to pick Les Mills in the 1974 New Zealand team for the Commonwealth Games in Christchurch. Had he been included it would have meant a unique family achievement for the Mills family. Les's wife Colleen was in the New Zealand track and field team, as were their two children, Donna and Phillip. In the event, Les Mills's best shot-put distances of that season would have placed him fifth at the Games. He did television commentary instead.

8 Having to read overseas newspapers in the 1930s and see the great horse Phar Lap being called an Australian horse when all along New Zealanders knew he had been born in South Canterbury.

9 Losing 3–12 to Pakistan in a World Cup hockey match in 1981. (After winning the gold medal at the 1976 Olympics New Zealanders felt their team was still a force to be reckoned with at a solid international level. This huge defeat changed those ideas.)

10 Rugby league faith was also severely undermined in 1972 when New Zealand began its World Cup campaign at the Parc des Princes Stadium in Paris but crashed to Great Britain by 53 points to 19. (Losses of that magnitude are very tough for rugby league fans to accept, especially as rugby union folk are always quick to remind league followers that the All Blacks never, ever, lost tests by such huge scores.)

So much for the top ten. Others that could come into this category include the early retirement of Peter Snell in 1965, the felling of Ewen Chatfield by an English bowler in a cricket test in Auckland in 1975, the failure of the New Zealand rowing eight to win a medal at the 1984 Olympic Games in Los Angeles, and the tragic car crash in South Africa in 1963 that killed the wife and children of the South African test cricketer Peter Carlstein and had a profound effect on New Zealanders. He was on tour in New Zealand at the time.

As for the bizarre side of New Zealand sport and how it relates to this book, it would be difficult to compile a top ten list of bizarre sporting incidents. Events of that nature cannot, I believe, be categorised. They are, however, included in the pages that follow. I have also interspersed the text with quiz questions designed to test the deeply knowledgeable sports fan with a penchant for the trivial side of sport. I hope you enjoy the tall tales and true of New Zealand sport as they unfold in the following pages. And maybe, on the way, a few arguments may be settled by what is written — or new ones started.

Athletics

A New Zealander played a major part in one of the technical developments of modern track and field. This sequence of photos shows John Delamere of Waikato and Auckland demonstrating his somersault long-jump technique which he worked on while studying at Washington State University. John could match his previous best distances, but eventually the style faded out of the sport.

Call of Nature

As all marathon runners know, the performing of all one's urgent physical necessities before a long race is vitally important to a pleasant and uncomplicated run. At a marathon start a common sight is athletes queuing up at portable toilets for a last nervous release of natural bodily waste. Even if one misses that chance, many are the opportunities along the way to hop over a fence and duck behind a hedge or tree — or anywhere — to ensure that the rest of the run is simple and comfortable.

But stop a minute. Consider the problem if you are running the Olympic or Commonwealth Games marathon and there is a big crowd cramming every inch of the way — and suddenly nature demands an urgent visit.

That was precisely the problem faced by one of New Zealand's top marathon men a few years back. He had paid several 'visits', but straight after the starting gun had gone he felt a desperate need to go again. But the race of his life was on. What could he do?

What he did was not pleasant as it happened. The Kiwi runner fouled himself. Afterwards he was to say there was no alternative. There were 70,000 people watching and millions more on television. And he was very nervous and highly strung. So he ran on in the race not heeding the damage acidic contents of human waste can do to sensitive leg skin. Eventually the sharp edge of pain on his upper thighs and backside told him chafing was occurring. Still he ran on. Many people, after all, had made sacrifices for

him to be representing New Zealand at the Games. He felt he could not let them down.

When our man finished the race over two hours later, his time was way outside what he was capable of in New Zealand. And there were people at home listening and watching who rubbished his effort. From afar it looked like another case of an athlete touring away and enjoying rather too much of the good life instead of knuckling down to training and discipline.

But the real story of the race was desperately sad for the New Zealander. By the time he finished the race, the insides of his legs were rubbed red and raw, the skin of his upper thighs was exposed and he was in the most excruciating pain. His teammates helped him away from the finish line as he could not support himself. It was days before he could venture outdoors again on his feet.

Our man's name is not on the scroll of winners from the Olympic or Commonwealth Games, but I have no doubt that his 'run' was one of the greatest of this country's unheralded moments of sporting courage.

Question: Where was John Walker when he received the 1976 Sportsman of the Year Award?

Answer: He was in bed at Middlemore Hospital recovering from an appendicitis operation.

Tragic Twins

One of the most tragic stories in New Zealand sporting history concerns a pair of identical twins, Bernice and Doreen Lumley. Born in 1922, the girls weighed only 62 pounds between them at birth. Later they both suffered from flat feet yet grew up to be fine track sprinters. Doreen, in particular, was very fast. Her sister Bernice was two or three yards slower.

Doreen had a great day at Carlaw Park in March of 1939. Running on a rough grass track that was cut out of the rugby league field, she beat the five times Empire gold medallist from Australia, Decima Norman. Naturally the crowd was delighted, and their delight turned to utter joy when it was announced that Doreen Lumley's time had in fact equalled the world record for the 100 yards.

Sadly, the great potential exhibited by the seventeen-year-old that day was never fully realised. Doreen and Bernice, the flying twins, were killed together in a car accident at Mt Wellington seven months later.

Mystery . . .

On a hot August afternoon the spectators at the 1978 Commonwealth Games in Edmonton waited expectantly for the 5000-metres final to begin. Kiwi hopes that day were firmly fixed on the in-form Rod Dixon. Henry Rono, the world record holder, was in the field, but with both John Walker and Dick Quax injured, there was a great opportunity for Dixon to get in amongst the medals — even to win gold.

From my TV commentary position I could easily identify the leading contenders as they limbered up for the race — Rono and his fellow Kenyan Michael Musyoki, Englishmen Nick Rose and Brendan Foster — but I couldn't spot the black vest of Dixon. Probably he was still track-suited, hidden amongst the athletes and officials who were milling about near the start. But as race-time approached, mild surprise turned to puzzlement and then apprehension. Where *was* Dixon?

Well, Dixon as I later discovered, was in the midst of a behind-the-scenes drama that was taking place in the athletes' changing-area and the warm-up track behind the main stadium.

Dixon had arrived at the changing rooms in the company of his coaches, Arch Jelley and Les Mills, along with Alan Thurlow, another New Zealander who had made it to the final. There was plenty of time for a relaxed and careful build-up to the race, and the two runners had gone out to jog and exercise on the warm-up track. Access to this area was denied to the public and only a few curious onlookers watched through a wire-netting fence as the athletes went through their preparations.

Dixon was in an old pair of running shoes, intending to appear in the race in a brand new pair of shoes which he had left inside the changing-room, in a bag with two other pairs of different sizes. Once his pre-race routine was complete, Dixon returned to the changing-room and donned his New Zealand shirt, shorts, running number and socks. Then he looked for his new shoes. As he tells it, he was not immediately concerned when the shoes were not where he had put them though the other two pairs were. Perhaps his coaches were holding them, he thought. He called to Mills, who went to ask Jelley.

The shoes could not be far away, thought Dixon, as there had only been three other athletes in the changing-room when the New Zealanders had arrived. Those three, Africans from other events, had since left the room. But when Jelley called back to Mills that the shoes were not with either him or Thurlow, a feeling of concern began to rise for the first time. Before a big race, like any athlete, Rod Dixon likes his thinking to be clear and undistracted. But the shoes were gone! And race-time was only minutes away.

Inside the stadium the Canadian crowd, basking in the warm sun with high expectancy of again seeing the great Henry Rono run, knew nothing of the unfolding events away from their view. Only the few hundred New Zealanders in the stadium, who natu-rally were trying to spot Dixon, were getting anxious.

Next came a call on the public address system for anyone who 'might have picked up New Zealand gear-bag number 35 to return it immediately to the athletes' room'. Now I *knew* some-thing was up. It was past the race start-time and no Dixon had appeared. The other starters had been called up to the start line twice, only to back off in confusion when told there would be a slight delay.

Another call came on the public address system. 'Would Phillip Mills of New Zealand please bring his run-ning gear to the athletes' changing area.' This was Les Mills calling to his son, of approximately the same physi-cal stature as Dixon, to urgently bring some alternate shoes. By now, every-one was aware of the sensation that Dixon was not there and most of us presumed he had lost his running gear. Kiwis in the crowd sprang into action. From the athletes' section of the grandstand a New Zealand singlet was thrown down to the trackside, and Barbara Beable, the pen-tathelete, was seen running down the steps with a pair of shoes in her hands. New Zealanders in the crowd, led by athletics writer Spencer Jolly, told officials that, should the race begin without Dixon, they would all jump the fence and lie on the track to prevent the race going ahead. And they meant it!

After a delay that seemed hours, but which was in reality about ten min-utes, a huge cheer went up from the crowd as Rod Dixon raced out of the changing room and on to the track. But from his bustling manner as he raced towards the other starters it was obvi-ous that he was in great distress, and in no sort of state to challenge the great Rono.

The gun sounded and the 5000-metres race started. After only a lap or two it was obvious Rod Dixon was not going to challenge the leaders, despite the screamed encouragement of the New Zealanders there. He gradually slid back in the field and even, with four laps to go, held his hands wide, palms upward, in a gesture of despair to his New Zealand fans, both at the track and watching live on television at home.

It was a sensation both confusing and disappointing to Dixon's many admirers, and when Henry Rono won comfortably, with Musyoki second and Foster third, most New Zealanders could not have cared less. They wanted answers to questions. Why was Dixon late on to the track? How could he have forgotten his gear? Had he lost his shoes?

The mystery has no solution. I later asked Les Mills to take me through the incident, but he could offer no explanation. He had been over the sequence of events with Dixon and Jelley many times. The shoes, lying in a box alongside two other pairs, simply disappeared, never to be seen again. To this day no one knows who took them or why.

With his correct footwear gone, replaced by an unfamiliar fitting, and his mind in turmoil as a result of the whole affair, so too did Rod Dixon's chances of a gold medal disappear into nothingness.

Question: *When Jack Lovelock won his gold medal in the 1500 metres at the 1936 Olympic Games, what did he have in common (apart from the distance of the race) with John Davies of New Zealand when he came third in the 1500 metres at Tokyo in 1964?*

Answer: *They both wore the same number — 467.*

Whoops!

My good friend John Davies will not mind, I am sure, if he is reminded of his quote during a live telecast from the Christchurch Commonwealth Games in 1974.

Davies: 'No wonder this Filbert Bayi has great speed. When he was out training as a boy in Tanzania, he used to be chased in the jungles by tigers!'

Five minutes later, the switchboards at television studios all over New Zealand were bombarded by people phoning up, all with the same message. 'Tell that Davies, there are no tigers in Africa!'

Question: *When New Zealander Cecil Matthews won his two gold gedals on the track at the 1938 Empire Games in Sydney, what was peculiar about the track he ran on?*

Answer: *It was odd-shaped. It was cut from the grass surface of the Sydney Cricket Ground and matched the circular nature of the field and its grandstand. It had only a short straight section and was best described at the time as being a 'misshapen D' in design. Sprints were run diagonally across the turf on another track, as they also were at the Empire Games at Eden Park in 1950.*

Storm in a Tokyo Teacup

What a fuss, a stupid fuss, was made in 1964 by some stuffy stay-at-home New Zealanders over an incident at the closing ceremony of the 1964 Olympic Games in Tokyo. The whole story bears the mark of boring people being upset by others having innocent fun in a manner which they (the boring ones) judged offensive.

The version I give is that recounted to me by one of the New Zealanders involved in the 'incident'. Picture the scene. The competitions are all over. The Olympic flag has been lowered and

Was the Emperor of Japan shocked by what he saw at the closing ceremony of the 1964 Olympic Games? Or was he pleased that the New Zealanders were thanking him in the Japanese way?

Below The infamous 'bowing' incident. Was this honourable behaviour or crass bad manners?

drummed out of the stadium. The flame has been dimmed and the invitation to attend the next Games has beenannounced to all present. The ceremonials are completed and the athletes of the world take over in a marvellous atmosphere of international goodwill and friendship. They dance to the music as it blares around the stadium and 100,000 Japanese in the crowd thunder their applause at the fun.

In the crush of athletes a group of New Zealanders, arm in arm, have their fun with a race around the track. It may not be as funny as the Keystone Cops but it is pure fun.

On their journey around the track the athletes arrive at the front of the royal box and, in keeping with what is done millions of times by everyone, every day in that country, the New Zealanders form a line and bow to the Emperor. That is what one does to say 'thank you' in Japan.

Having done that and seen the beams of smiles from everyone in return, the New Zealanders continue their crazy race around the track.

The ceremony was being telecast live all over Japan and around the world, but in the hubbub the TV cameras had missed the Kiwi gesture to the royal box. Thus the New Zealanders were asked to repeat the bow for TV. This they did and then once more resumed their riotous journey around the stadium.

My informant tells me that the bowing was received with nothing but absolute delight by the Japanese people, both royal and ordinary. Nowhere was there a whisper of controversy. Far from it. The Japanese people seemed delighted that someone was attempting their way of doing things.

Not so at home in New Zealand. The next day newspapers were yelling headlines at how New Zealanders had insulted Japanese royalty by mocking the dignity of the bowing ceremony. What an almighty fuss broke out! This and that New Zealand leader had his say. Comments were made on declining standards of behaviour, questions were asked as to why the 'lampooning' and 'burlesque' bow had been done.

To the athletes involved it was the fuss not the incident that became the joke. They say that not one word of censure came from any Japanese people about the incident. Indeed, they say no mention at all of the event came until they reached home and suddenly found themselves being closely questioned about something they regarded as being just a slice of the gaiety of the whole closing ceremony.

Time, I suppose, has cooled the issue. But in 1964 it was a big, big talking point in New Zealand. But nowhere else it seems. Now, in the 1990s, those that took part and who just wanted to say 'thank you' in a Japanese way are still bewildered by the storm of protest that was made by people who perhaps did not fully understand the way honour is paid to a host or hostess in Japan.

Beaten by the Clock

There are several stories along the lines of this one where the expectations of sporting officials before an event were not matched later by the event's actual outcome. Here is one of those yarns.

At the peak of Peter Snell's time as the top competing athlete in New Zealand he was invited to run in Opunake in Taranaki. Also invited to the country meeting were Snell's great New Zealand rival, John Davies of Tokoroa, and several other leading runners from around the North Island.

For the one-mile race that was to feature the great Snell, a crowd of nearly everyone in tiny Opunake turned out. The prize for the race was displayed on a table among the cups and trophies for other events.

It seems that Snell, Davies and company were to run for the honour of winning an impressive mantle clock. There, for all to see beforehand, was the clock on the table.

Soon enough the event took place and the crowd leaned forward as the field of top milers swept around their four circuits of the track. The cheering reached its crescendo as the field turned into the finishing straight for the last time. In the race to the tape it was in fact John Davies who out-sprinted Snell to cause a major upset and win.

Just how big an upset it was was confirmed later for John Davies when he was presented with the mantle clock. As the applause for the presentation died away Davies looked down proudly at his prize. There, engraved on to a silver plaque and screwed firmly into the face of the clock (and obviously done days before) was an inscription which read something like — 'To Peter Snell, on the occasion of his victory in the Opunake One-Mile Race.'

It seems someone's pre-race confidence in Snell was not borne out by the actuality of events!

Out of His Tree

In 1986 the New Zealand Amateur Athletics Association sent a team to New Caledonia for a week of competition. Apparently, the happy band of athletes enjoyed themselves hugely and most of them competed well.

But, sad to say, one competitor was not able to produce a top-class performance. The story goes that the intrepid Kiwi athlete, in a spirit of fun, decided to climb a nearby coconut tree. This is apparently great fun and can be achieved with reasonable ease even by New Zealand athletes who obviously do not have much experience of the feat!

The bizarre twist to this tale is that, while reaching out to complete the climb, the IKA (Intrepid Kiwi Athlete) overstretched a leg, pulling a hamstring muscle. Soon it was established that the climb would cost this athlete the total fitness required for the international competition in track and field — the main reason for his being there.

I do not doubt that the IKA later became the EKA (Embarrassed Kiwi Athlete). I cannot recall many instances of international sportsmen being injured while climbing coconut trees!

First Woman Marathon Runner

In recent years New Zealand has established a proud record in marathon running. Our athletes have performed wonders in this event, with women outscoring men in terms of international success.

People like Ann Audain, Allison Roe, Lorraine Moller, Mary O'Connor and Ngaire Drake all secured great wins in the 1980s and have made New Zealand women marathon runners respected and feared worldwide.

But that respect was not always present for New Zealand women athletes who favoured running long distances. In 1964 an Auckland housewife, Mrs Mildred Sampson, applied to the Owairaka Athletic Club to run in their annual marathon but her entry was officially turned down. At the time Millie Sampson was New Zealand's leading woman runner of long events but apparently it was not felt 'right' for her to run in the marathon race with men.

But a determined Millie turned up at the start line on race day and took off in pursuit of her goal — to finish a marathon.

Because she ran without the formal sanction of the race committee, you could say that her effort on the day, 21 July 1964, was unofficial. But brave Millie ran on . . .

She eventually finished with a time of 3 hours 19 minutes 33 seconds, a fantastic effort. Further elation followed when it was discovered that her time was a world best for a woman runner over the 26 mile and 385 yard journey.

That Millie Sampson was able to overcome her initial rejection from the race and run in world-record time was perhaps the example that all New Zealand women runners needed. Following her proud effort other runners gained the confidence to achieve many great feats in years to come.

BOXING

All Black Bruising

The 1921 final of the New Zealand amateur heavyweight boxing championship was remarkable for the fact that both contestants were All Blacks — or rather they soon became All Blacks. (Perhaps there were a few rugby selectors in the crowd that night!) Brian McCleary beat Maurice Brownlie on points, though it was the latter who received his rugby call-up the following year. Both men toured Britain with the All Blacks in 1924–5, though by then McCleary had won and lost the New Zealand professional boxing title.

His conqueror was the tough Gisborne heavyweight Tom Heeney. It was reckoned a classic contest, though it ended with McCleary being rushed to hospital where his condition was soon reported to be critical. He recovered, however, and continued boxing until 1927. His defeat was no disgrace, it must be said, for Heeney later challenged Gene Tunney for the world heavyweight title.

Question: Who were the four All Blacks to win the New Zealand amateur heavyweight boxing title?

Answer: Brian McCleary — champion in 1920 and 1921; an All Black in 1924–25.
Arch McCormick — champion in 1922 and 1923; an All Black in 1925.
Maurice McHugh — champion in 1938; an All Black in 1949.
Kevin Skinner — champion in 1947; an All Black from 1949 to 1956.

Death in the Ring

The sport of boxing has a history of being well controlled in this country. It is a fine discipline when it is closely and safely supervised. And because of its strict medical scrutiny and closely observed rules boxing has generally ridden over the bad publicity and calls for abolition that have inevitably arisen when fighters have lost their lives pursuing man's basic pugnacity.

However, the cause of boxing was not helped by this small notice, which appeared in a Greymouth newspaper in October 1933:

Last night a young professional, Bert Lowe, collapsed during a bout and died in Grey Hospital. Death was due to a haemorrhage of the brain. The bout, while it lasted, was one of the best seen in Greymouth for many years.

Small comfort to the relatives of Mr Lowe!

Michener's Mistake

Hands up those who read that magnificent book *The Covenant* by James A. Michener and marvelled at the depth of research behind it. I scoffed when the novel reached the passage of time where the Springbok team were to travel to New Zealand to play rugby. There Michener quotes the great New Zealand boxer Tom Heeney as having been a footballer of note and having played against the Springboks.

A trip to a dusty bookshelf in my garage proved Mr Michener's research to be correct. Tom Heeney, later to fight Gene Tunney for the world heavyweight boxing title, was in 1921 simply a tough young tyke from Gisborne. He certainly was a rugby player, and good enough to play for Poverty Bay/East Coast against the first Springbok touring team in New Zealand. It was only later that Heeney forsook his football boots for boxing gloves.

I can, however, claim one victory over Michener's research team. While on one page he claims correctly that Heeney played for Poverty Bay/East Coast against the touring team, one only has to turn the page (page 693 in my copy!) to see reference to the third test of 1921 being played at Wellington, also a correct fact. Michener has the score of the

Tom Heeney, the man they called 'The Hard Rock from Down Under'. To be sure, he was a great boxer — but he was not ever an All Black.

Memories

Paddy McNally was one of the great characters of New Zealand boxing. During the 1950s and 60s Paddy was a hard-hitting, hard-living but lovable rogue who won several New Zealand championships and who enjoyed nothing more than his career in boxing and the millions of memories his many fights gave him.

As befitting a friendly chap, Paddy was never short of a mate or three to drink with and share his humour and wistful recollections of the glory days of his past.

In the years after his retirement from active fighting, Paddy and his mates always went to the New Zealand amateur boxing championships. Wherever the championships were held Paddy, his brother Joe, and a host of friends would always travel to enjoy the contests in the ring and the camaraderie out of it.

When Paddy McNally died at an early age, naturally his mates were shocked and saddened — as were fight fans around New Zealand who had enjoyed his talent and his fun.

His brother Joe also missed him. But there was no time to look back sadly at the life of Paddy McNally. At the first New Zealand amateur boxing championships after his death Paddy's ashes were solemnly carried to the venue of the fights. There in their container they were displayed in an appropriate place so that homage to Paddy's memory could be suitably paid.

game true to life (0–0) and recalls accurately that the day was atrociously wet and the ground at Athletic Park very muddy. But he goes one step too far. In his story, as the players leave the field after the test match, Michener quotes Tom Heeney as saying, 'We didn't beat you Springboks, but by gum we nearly did.' There the great writer is wrong. Tom Heeney (the 'Hard Rock from Down Under') might have played for his home province but he never graced the All Black rugby team.

CRICKET

Baffling Bob Bitmead

In recent years cricketing purists have wondered about the unorthodox nature of some of the bowling actions of players in the world of cricket.

The cheek of those Aussies! Dennis Lillee bowls to the maximum slip field available in a test in Auckland against New Zealand in 1977. At the wicket for this picture, which was staged for a cricket magazine cover, are those two stalwarts of New Zealand's tailend, Ewen Chatfield *(facing)* and Peter Petherick. *Photograph:* New Zealand Herald

Some internationals, like Fred Trueman, Ray Lindwall and Dennis Lillee, had superbly smooth approaches to the wicket and immaculate delivery actions. Others, like the Australian Max ('Tangles') Walker and New Zealanders Bob Cunis and Lance Cairns had great success in the game despite having bowling actions that were a coach's nightmare.

Of all the bowlers who have played cricket internationally in New Zealand, none would approach the 1967 Australian tourist Bob Bitmead. His bowling action was a whirling tangle of arms and legs and, to my way of thinking, the most crazily unorthodox ever seen in New Zealand. Yet he was a specialist bowler who was very nearly a full Australian test player.

When he was in New Zealand in 1967 Bitmead described his action as 'The Baffle' and suggested light-heartedly that young people should copy it as a new dance craze. Bitmead was a slow left-arm bowler who approached the wicket from just a few paces of run-up. When he was at the delivery stride his arms and legs went into a marionette-like flurry that is actually very difficult to describe. The end result was a ball

delivered from a crab-like stance with the left arm coming over to the release point on the left foot, which purists will tell you is not the 'correct' way.

The New Zealand players Bevan Congdon and Dick Motz may recall baffling Bob Bitmead. They were his two wickets, secured at Carisbrook in Dunedin in the Victorian's only international appearance, during the tour of 1967.

Bless Me!

I wonder how the Reverend E. O. Blamires felt towards his God after the second test match in the 1923–4 cricket series against Australia. The good Reverend had thumped the visitors for 67 when he played for his province, Otago, against them. When weighed up with an innings of 133 that he had earlier hit for Otago against Canterbury, the New Zealand selectors felt it was time the cricketing cleric moved up a notch to the exalted status of representing his country.

Alas for the Rev. Blamires, his debut for New Zealand was not a happy one. Far from it. Batting at number 3 he fell to Charlie McCartney's bowling in the first innings and to Sam Everett's in the second. On both occasions his score was the dreaded nought!

The Reverend was never asked to play for his country again. The oaths he uttered, whether biblically printable or otherwise, at his dreaded pair of ducks are not recorded.

Bula

Pity the small boys who operated the cricket scoreboards of New Zealand during the three Fijian cricket tours after the Second World War. The young lads who alter the scores at cricket matches, day in day out, have done the game a great service. I draw your attention to the Fijian tours of 1947–8, 1953–4 and 1961–2 because the scoreboard attendants in those years had to contemplate the formidable name of Bulamainavaleniveivakabulaimaina-volakebalao as a full-blooded member of the touring party. Luckily, the first four letters of his name abbreviated nicely to scoreboard and scorebook length. Bula they called him — which

is, of course, the same word as the cheery, smiling greeting one gets a dozen times every day in those sunny Fijian islands.

In those seasons Bula was a great treat for New Zealand cricket fans, as he of the forty-four letter name also knew how to abbreviate his times at the wicket to only the most exciting hitting.

Bula was a striker of sixes of the most prodigious lengths. To him it was nothing to loft the ball out of the ground not once, twice, but six and seven times in his innings. Consider

these scores as he raced to 1000 runs in New Zealand in a matter of weeks in 1947–8: 77 and 53 not out (9 sixes in the match) against Waikato; 44 and 36 v. Auckland; 88 v. Wellington; 63 and 120 v. Canterbury; 8 v. Poverty Bay.

Bula's next tour was not quite as successful but again Canterbury's bowlers suffered. He hit 8 sixes and 5 fours as he thundered to 102 in only 63 minutes. Poor Canterbury! When Bula came back in 1961–2 he was older and not scoring so freely. But still the Canterbury bowlers reeled from a thunderous assault. He made 118, his third century in Christ-church, in three tours.

Bula had an amazingly stoical facial exterior. No matter how hard he thumped the opposition attack and no matter how much he must have enjoyed seeing their bowling fly high and wide out of reach of everyone, the big Fijian never once hinted at a smile. To Bula it seemed a very serious business indeed.

The other peculiarity about Bula was that he batted every innings in the Fijian men's skirt — the sulu — and bare feet, another part of his personality that attracted New Zealanders in their thousands to see him and his fellow countrymen play.

Incidentally, his long, long, surname came from the story of how the joyous news of his birth was the key to his grandfather's rapid recovery from a serious illness. The Fijian meaning of the name relates to Bula's grandfather 'returning alive from Navoa Hospital at Lakemba Island in the Lau group'.

And just for the record, Bula's Christian names were Ilikena Lasarusa — making his whole name fifty-nine letters long. Small wonder it

It's doubtful whether any batsman in New Zealand cricketing history was as popular as Peter Coman of Canterbury. In the 1970s Coman had a swing at anything going: a lot of the time he connected. Ask the Pakistani team of 1973! *Photograph:* New Zealand Truth

was shortened to ease the burden of all those keen young scoreboard boys!

Coman's Welcome

What a way to welcome a cricket team to New Zealand! The 1973 Pakistani tourists had arrived downcast at having lost three straight tests to Australia in the previous two-and-a-half weeks.

They must have looked to New Zealand to provide some respite from the batterings they had taken in Australia from the likes of Lillee, Walker, the Chappell brothers and Rodney Marsh. But if the Pakistanis did eventually win their test series with New Zealand 1–0, Peter Coman of Canterbury was one New Zealander who must have un-nerved them and made them think they were in for more of what the Australians had given them.

After being in New Zealand for only nine hours the Pakistan team took to the field against Canterbury and the big fast bowler Safraz Nawaz took the new ball. He bounded in to bowl to the Canterbury opener Peter Coman and in what was probably an act of intimidation bounced the first ball high at the batsman's head.

Coman was nothing if not instinctive and flamboyant. Leaning foward he assumed the hooking position and hit a superb shot that sent the ball flying over the square leg boundary for six. I can recall listening to the radio commentary at home and hearing the broadcasters' voices raised in utter surprise at Coman's audacity. Two balls later Safraz again tried to bounce the ball to Coman. Again the curly-headed Cantabrian hooked, again the crowd roared, the commentators gasped, and again a six was signalled.

As I recall, before the end of the over a swathing cut from Coman had sent another ball from Safraz crashing into the fence for four, which leaves me wondering just what the Pakistanis had thought they had struck. Surely no tour ever began in such a manner, with a prized fast bowler being 'carted' about by a local who had little or no international reputation.

Peter Coman was in fact a batting freak. He loved nothing more than to thump the reputations of all the tear-away fast bowlers he could find. True, he did not always succeed and often

the big crowds who came especially to see him play were disappointed, but he did make several first-class centuries, and once made 266 in a Christchurch senior-club match on a single Saturday afternoon.

Debut

Fans have always been fascinated to watch the international debut of a rising new star. So when Aucklander Rodney Redmond made his test match debut at Eden Park in 1973 against Pakistan, the interest generated amongst his fellow Aucklanders was enormous.

With a big, boisterous crowd roaring its approval of their local son, Redmond came out to bat and flayed the Pakistani bowlers to all corners of the field. He eventually reached 107, which made him, after Jack Mills and Bruce Taylor, only the third Kiwi batsman to make a century in his first test

Rodney Redmond came out swinging in his only test match and thumped the Pakistani bowlers for 107 and 56. Sadly, he was not needed again at test level.

A slow starter in test cricket, John Parker eventually became one of the most popular subjects for Kiwi sideline barracking. His critics forgot he was, in the end, a topline batsman.

match. All three, incidentally, were left-handers.

At one point of his innings Redmond hit five successive fours to rapturous applause. At this point all of New Zealand believed a brilliant new batsman had been found who would benefit the game for years to come. Redmond confirmed this belief with a second innings of 56, creating the highest tally of any New Zealander in his first test.

Rodney Redmond qualifies for this book because it transpired that his first test match against Pakistan, which contained so many good things, was also his last.

Redmond toured England later that same year with the New Zealand team. He pressed hard for a test place as opening batsman but one did not come his way. His form was only moderate and he completed the tour with an

average a little over 28 runs per innings. Despite scores of 65, 57 and 79 in his first three innings against county sides, he never quite hit enough runs to earn a place in the tests. After that tour and in later seasons Rodney Redmond's form fluctuated, and his availability for first-class cricket was not always certain. Eventually he was lost to the New Zealand cricketing scene, and now he is mainly remembered as the dashing opening batsman who was never allowed, by circumstances or selection, to confirm the form shown in his only test match.

If Rodney Redmond was the most successful New Zealand batsman on his test debut, the palm for perhaps the most personally disastrous beginning in test cricket could be awarded to that redoubtable batsman of the same era, John Parker.

Parker was a Northern Districts opener of style and elegance who complemented his play in New Zealand with good tallies of runs in England as a member of the Worcestershire county side.

Eventually Parker's early promise as a batsman saw him elevated to full test honours. He was, one presumes, full of hope for a good beginning to his test career when the day dawned in Wellington for the first test between New Zealand and the Pakistan touring team in 1973 (the same team that Rodney Redmond was to face).

The history of cricket is littered with the names of famous players selected for their batting who have fallen to a 'duck' on their test debuts. Len Hutton, Victor Trumper, Ken Barrington, Mike Brearley and Glenn Turner are just some who have walked on to their first test arena full of ambition and desire only to return moments later with a nought against their name and sympathy their only solace.

Poor John Parker did not even get their chance of success. Fielding before lunch on the first day, he was struck on the hand by a strongly hit shot from the Pakistani opener Sadiq Mohammed. The New Zealander retired in great pain to the dressing room where a fracture was diagnosed. Thus, only hours into his test cricket career, John Parker was invalided out of the game, actually taking no further part in any of the five days.

For the record, it was four months before he did play test cricket again, and when he did begin, John Parker was not a raging success. Scores of 2, 6, 3, 8 and 4 were agonisingly chipped off the England bowlers. Only in the later years of his career did the popular Parker put his early disappointments behind him and more securely cement his place in the New Zealand test team.

Ducks Galore

There is no question that the scoring of a 'duck' at cricket is some kind of sporting disaster. But it is a disaster usually tinged with rueful humour. The traditional vision of a batsman having been dismissed without scoring is that of a man (or woman) returning to the pavilion with a sheepish grin across the face, accompanied by a shrug of the shoulders and an inner determination to do better things next time.

There have been many ducks scored in the history of New Zealand cricket. To mention them all would occupy far

too many pages. But a study of the disappointments and disasters of New Zealand sport must record some of the more famous ducks with which the Kiwi game has been graced.

In 1930, New Zealand played its first official test match against England at Lancaster Park in Christchurch. The New Zealand first innings began disastrously and soon the Kiwis were 7 wickets down for only 21 runs. There was a recovery of sorts, till the team was all out for 112. Of the ducks scored that day the 'honour' of recording the very first by a New Zealander in a test actually went to the team's captain, Tom Lowry.

Worse befell other players in the team. Both K. C. James, the wicket-

Two of Hawke's Bay's best, Tom Lowry and Maurice Brownlie, who captained their country at its two most popular sports. But this pair of talented sportsmen feature in this book for other reasons: Lowry, because he was the first New Zealander to make a duck in a cricket test match, and Brownlie as the beaten finalist in the New Zealand heavyweight boxing final of 1921.

When young Glenn Turner played his first test innings at Auckland against the West Indies he was out to two of the greatest players of all time . . . c Sobers, b Hall . . . 0. But in fourteen further years of test cricket he was never again dismissed for nought.

The highest total of ducks by New Zealanders in one test match is 8, including three sets of pairs in the disastrous second test v. England at Eden Park in Auckland in 1955. Wicketkeeper Ian Colquhoun was out twice to the same catching position off the same bowler in that game! His dismissals, both first ball, assisted the England spinner Bob Appleyard to twice be on a hat trick.

On the same ground eight years later, Mike Shrimpton fared only marginally better in a test against South Africa. He was out twice for nought, but in total faced three balls!

Against India at Wellington in 1980-1 Gary Troup scored ducks at the lowest possible 'rate'. The big Aucklander fell to a duck at the end of both New

keeper, and F. T. Badcock, the fast bowler, fell to ducks in the first innings and then again in the second! Thus was set a tradition of 'pairs' (or spectacles) being scored in test matches, a tradition that has touched some of the more prominent New Zealand players of the past as well as of modern times.

The very talented Wellington fast bowler of the fifties and sixties, Bob Blair, himself a most attractive batsman (but obviously only when things were going right!) fell to ducks in his test career no fewer than 12 times, including 3 pairs. Dick Motz also made 12 ducks in tests. Blair qualifies as the top duck exponent since he batted 34 times in tests to Motz's 56.

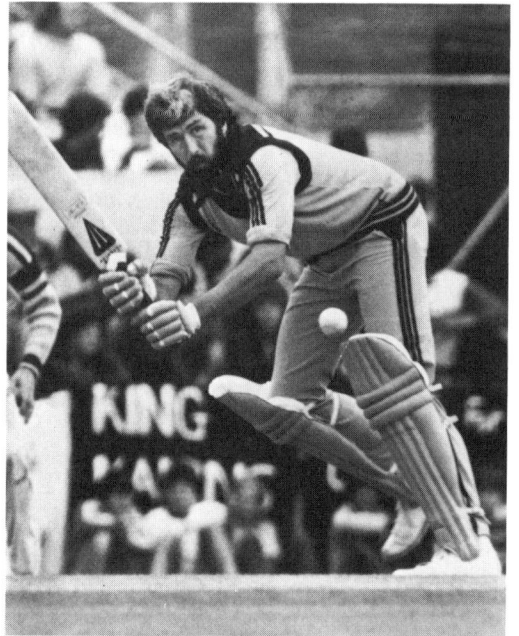

Did any batsman ever have a longer wait to score a 'golden' duck than John Morrison? While the rain fell he waited two-and-a-half days to bat, only to fall to the first ball of a test match. *Photograph by Ross Setford*

Zealand innings, out first ball both times. This was only the third occasion that any test player of any country had fallen to a 'golden' pair.

Ducks by prominent batsmen when runs in abundance would have been preferable have often landed Kiwi cricket in deep trouble. When Mike Shrimpton (sorry to mention you again, Mike!) scored a duck against England in 1966, again at Eden Park, his opening partner Terry Jarvis also fell for no score. New Zealand were 2 down for none!

Terry Jarvis also featured among the ducks at Wellington in 1973. Playing against Pakistan in the first test Jarvis scored a pair, but when Bevan Congdon and Brian Hastings also fell for ducks in the second innings, New Zealand were 3 down for 11. With the top three batsmen all showing ducks on the scoreboard and John Parker unable to bat because of njury, things could not have been much worse for the Kiwis. Only resolute batting by Mark Burgess and Glenn Turner saved the test match from defeat.

Turner himself had begun from humble beginnings as a test player. In his debut international, against the West Indies in 1969, he fell for a duck in his first innings, though he could take consolation in the fact that it took two of the world's greatest players, Gary Sobers and Wesley Hall, to dismiss him (caught Sobers bowled Hall: 0). Great success followed Glenn Turner after that game. He never again fell for a duck in a test match.

Turner is now a television commentator and so is another former test player, John Morrison. Morrison can lay claim to a test duck that was out of the ordinary. He was included in the New Zealand team for the second test against England at Lancaster Park in 1975. Unfortunately the Christchurch weather proved most uncooperative and the first day, and then the second, were completely washed out. After detailed discussions between the managers and a long mopping-up operation, play began after lunch on the third day.

John Morrison opened the batting for his country but snicked the first ball of the match, delivered by the England fast bowler Geoff Arnold, straight to Mike Hendrick at third slip.

The victorious Australian cricketers of 1946. So nice of them to play us in an offical test match after all those years when they were so near yet so far.

The catch was duly taken and Morrison journeyed back to the pavilion after surely the longest wait for the shortest innings on record!

I can attest to the absolute necessity to arrive early at a cricket test match. In 1974, on a hot Auckland summer's day, I decided that watching test cricket from the Eden Park Terrace would not be comfortable without a carton of cool ale to quench a parched throat. Right on the tick of 11 am on the first day of the second test between New Zealand and Australia I was hurrying up the steps of the outer-ground seating at Eden Park when I dropped my precious cargo of beer cans! As I bent to pick it all up, behind me Richard Hadlee bowled the first ball of the test to the Australian opener Keith Stackpole. The roar from the crowd soon told me my distraction had caused me to miss a neatly taken catch by John Parker in the slips. My first view of Stackpole was of him heading back to the grandstand having fallen for a 'golden' duck! His misery was compounded by his dismissal in the second innings for another duck.

Actually, that test produced what must be a record of sorts. Eighteen wickets fell on the first day alone, one man scored a century (Doug Walters), but seven players (four Australians and three New Zealanders) fell for ducks.

In test cricket L. S. M. (Lawrie) Miller of Central Districts and Wellington lays claim to one of test cricket's most enduring (and perhaps embarrassing) records. On the 1953–4 New Zealand tour of South Africa, Miller, usually a dogged and reliable batsman, ran into a patch of dreadful form with the bat. In the first test and in the first innings of the second test he achieved a start in each of his innings, scoring 13, 18 and 14. From then on that series was a scoring disaster for Miller.

In the second innings of the second test, batting admittedly with a severe chest injury, he made a duck. Because of his ailment he missed the next test. Recalled for the fourth test he succumbed twice to the guile of the spinner Hugh Tayfield and again in the first innings of the fifth test he was soon marched back to the pavilion — on each occasion with the dreaded zero next to his name. His four successive ducks thus became a feat equal to the world's worst consecutive test-batting effort.

Lawrie may have felt better after the1961–2 New Zealand tour of South Africa. From home he would have read of Dick Motz's poor batting form on the same grounds and pitches of South Africa. Motz managed 5 ducks in the five test series.

The statistics of noughts scored in test matches involving New Zealand make sombre reading for Kiwis. They show 37 instances of pairs being scored by New Zealand players compared with only 14 by all the opposition players.

In the past several seasons and tours there have been two additions to the 'club' of those New Zealand players who have made pairs in tests. John Bracewell joined in Hyderabad in November 1984 against Pakistan while Ken Rutherford joined with a flourish in Port of Spain, Trinidad in March 1985 when playing against the West Indies.

Rutherford was in his first test match. He batted only briefly in the first innings facing only a few deliveries before being dismissed but he was not so 'lucky' in his second 'dig'. The hapless Rutherford was run out for nought before he had faced a ball!

And if you are thinking that I have exhausted most of the variations of the stories of ducks, stay please for one more.

The first test between England and New Zealand in July 1983 at the Oval provided ducks with a difference. The match was originally a family honour for the Crowes of Auckland. Both the brothers, Martin and Jeff, made the New Zealand test team, only the fifth occasion that brothers had represented their country in a test match. Their pride must have changed to some sort of chagrin when, in the first innings, both brothers returned from the batting crease, dismissed without scoring. It did not take long for one wag to point out that both Crowes made 'ducks' and that the umpire that gave them out was 'Dickie' Bird!

Embarrassing!

For many years Kiwi cricket was given the cold shoulder by the cricket authorities of Australia. Then, in 1946, an official Australian touring team crossed over to play one test match with the New Zealanders. It might have been better if they hadn't bothered, for the consequent game was a huge embarrassment and disaster for the host nation.

Australia had brought a team on tour that contained such later stars as Keith Miller, Ray Lindwall, Ian Johnson and Don Tallon (all were making their third test debuts in the international). Interspersed with the youngsters were some of the 'greats' of the pre-war game; players like Lindsay Hassett, Bill O'Reilly, Sid Barnes and E. R. H. Toshak. All in all it was a formidable team that New Zealand faced at Wellington in the early months of 1946.

New Zealand's captain, Walter Hadlee, won the toss and chose to bat first on a rain-affected pitch. But after starting full of hope, the Kiwis were slumped in their dressing room shortly after lunch, all out for 42! Verdun Scott, the Auckland opener, top scored with 14.

Australia batted for the rest of the first day, passing the New Zealand score with only one wicket down. Admittedly the Australians' total first-innings score was not great, all out for 199. That was mainly because of some great fast bowling by Jack Cowie (6 wickets tor 40 runs).

When New Zealand began its second innings there were still reasonable hopes for a good showing by the Kiwi batsmen.

Alas, New Zealand wickets fell cheaply, at regular intervals, to Miller, Lindwall, O'Reilly and Toshak. Soon the home team were all out in their second innings and the game was over as an innings win to Australia.

New Zealand's second innings score was 54, an improvement of 12 on their first effort at the wicket. The team's total score of 96 over two innings still stood, in 1983, as the lowest total aggregate by any country in two completed innings of a test match.

In fact, the game was not awarded full test status until 1948. It was a heavy irony that, after being cold-shouldered by Australia for all those years, New Zealanders in the end could not have cared less, because of the disastrous result, if the match had not been given its major rating.

But as usual in any dark situation, humour abounds. A Nelson man, Temple Sutherland, was moved to summarise the New Zealand first innings score thus:

Ten for Forty-two: A Lament

TEN little wickets, guarded by our best eleven,
Anderson let Lindwall through — and 1 was down for 7.

NINE little wickets standing on the Basin green,
Skipper fell to Toshak, 2 down, the runs 15.

EIGHT little wickets, but I'm sorry to relate,
Toshak collected Wallace; 37 on the slate.

SEVEN little wickets when Scott of Auckland came,
But O'Reilly sent him homeward, the score, alas, the same.

SIX little wickets, and with Rowe, O'Reilly proved,
He could keep the batsmen moving — so the score remained unmoved.

FIVE little wickets, but O'Reilly never faltered,
Butterfield pokes his leg before, the score remains unaltered.

FOUR little wickets and O'Reilly to McRae, Hassett takes it single-handed, the score just stays that way.

THREE little wickets, New Zealand's 'thin red line',
Burke, leg before, bowled Toshak —
8 down for 39.

TWO little wickets wishing hard that there were more,
Toshak skittled Tindill — and 40 is the score.

ONE little wicket on which our hopes depend,
Tallon says 'Good-bye' to Cowie, and at 42 the end.

NO little wickets, but still a record score. We never made so little in so big a game before!

Fielding a Speciality

Picking players for a cricket team on the basis of their batting or bowling talent is standard practice. Even choosing a wicketkeeper for that specialist role alone, regardless of how badly he or she bats, is far from uncommon. It is the art of fielding that is more often than not forgotten in the rush to pack a side with batsmen or bowlers. A flush of good fielders can save a cricket team in the field many runs. Good handling off the ground, speed to the ball, good catching and accurate throwing can all change the course of a game.

While there have been many who have carved reputations for themselves as batsmen or bowlers, over the years I can recall no player, at least in test cricket, who made his whole career out of the art of good fielding. And yet at least one man made fielding his ticket to the top in provincial cricket.

I go back to 1888 for the beginnings of this story. In that year the sole Canterbury selector, Mr A. M. Olivier, caused a ripple in Christchurch cricketing circles by including a young man, T. W. Reese, in his team when the lad had no apparent form with bat or ball, nor was he a wicketkeeper. 'He's in because he can field,' replied Mr Olivier to all queries.

The young Tom Reese was delighted. He was a slim young man built along lines that enabled him to speedily pursue any hits to the outfield. His hands were secure for catching and his throwing strong and usually on target. It mattered little to him where he appeared in the batting order and he never worried if he was not called on to bowl. Reese knew his role to be a fieldsman and that alone.

Reese played in and out of the Canterbury team until the 1907 season. In all those years he never averaged double figures with the bat, nor did he bowl much. His worth to his team came from a high number of runs saved in the field. Some said he saved more runs than some of the specialist batsmen of the time made at the crease.

Tom Reese's place in cricket does not end with his unique career as a specialist fielder. When his active days were done he took to researching and writing about the early days of the game in New Zealand. In the end he compiled two volumes of New Zealand cricketing records that have proved invaluable to historians of the game over the years. His brother Dan proved to be a noteworthy player of the game as well, representing New Zealand as an all-rounder for over twenty years.

How times have changed! Can you imagine Martin Crowe inspecting the pitch in a pinstriped suit? But they did it like that in the good old days. Norman Yardley, the MCC captain (*left*), and Merv Wallace (Auckland) inspect the pitch prior to the start of the Auckland v. MCC game at Eden Park in 1947. *Photograph:* New Zealand Herald

Question: Which New Zealand batsman hit the MCC bowler David Allen for three sixes in one over in one of the 'unofficial' tests of 1961–2?

Answer: Dick Motz dished it out. His three sixes were part of an innings of 60. Mind you, Walter Hammond had hit three sixes in a row for England against New Zealand at Eden Park in 1933. He was on his way to a score of 336. The pitiful over for New Zealand was bowled by Jack Newman.

King Stops Play

When there was no play on the morning of the second day of the cricket match between MCC and New Zealand at Lord's in May 1937, it wasn't because of rain. Rather, both teams travelled across London to see the parade of the Coronation of King George VI — a case of reign stops play, I suppose.

Women's Cricket

In 1935 a women's cricket team from England, captained by Elizabeth Archdale, made the pioneering women's cricket tour down under. If the Englishwomen had hopes of getting tough opposition from New Zealand teams, they were sadly disappointed. The game of cricket in New Zealand had only recently been accepted as being proper for women. One of the principal objections from high-handed males, it seems, came from having to observe women in 'ungainly' fielding stances.

Fortunately, the brave women cricketers of New Zealand rose above such nonsense and formed their own association in 1934. England had already been in operation as a national body for eight years. So that first test in Christchurch, all those years ago, was an eagerly awaited experience for the small band of keen women cricketers in New Zealand. Sadly for the game and its early development, the New Zealand team was considerably weaker than had originally been thought.

New Zealand batted first on 16 February 1935, a sunny Saturday. Over 3000 onlookers came to watch, with curiosity, a test match played between teams from a sex that was previously only encouraged to make the tea at men's games.

A little over an hour after the start of play the New Zealand women were sitting stunned in their dressing room having all been dismissed in their first innings for only 44.

Although the fall of wickets was not in the record that I found of the New Zealand innings, it would seem from the low placement in the batting of the top scorer, Merle Hollis, that the New Zealand ladies were, for a time, heading for a far worse score than 44! But mighty Merle swung lustily and made 24 of the 39 runs that came off the bat.

Worse was to follow. England, when they batted, simply wiped the ungainly New Zealand bowlers out. All their batswomen (ugh! What a word! Actually, women say 'bats' when describing a player at the wicket) fared comfortably on the pitch and soon the runs were racing way ahead of the tiny New Zealand score.

The wicketkeeper, Betty Snowball, was unstoppable. On her own she raced past her century and was finally out for 189, still the highest score in a test match by women. Molly Hide scored 110 and Mary Child 86 not out. On the second day England declared at 503 for five, New Zealand at that point being 459 behind!

In their second innings the New Zealand women fared much better. They scraped through to 122, a very respectable score when one considers the fast and elusive English bowling. No fewer than five New Zealanders made double figures! England won in the end by an innings and 337 runs but the wide margin of defeat put back the chances of a New Zealand tour to England in the future. The Second World War intervened, but it was not until nineteen years later in 1954 that the New Zealand women's team again faced England in a test match.

Indeed it was thirty-seven years before New Zealand won a women's cricket test match against any country. That was in Melbourne in 1972 when the Kiwis tipped over the Aussies by 143 runs. That was certainly a far cry from the debacle of 1935 — a loss that paralleled some of the hidings our male players were also to take in the years to come!

Longest Over?

There was a most unusual method of obtaining a new ball in the cricket match between New Zealand and the MCC at Carisbrook in Dunedin in 1936. The MCC, under the excellent captaincy of Errol Holmes, was a strong touring team and as it prepared for the first 'unofficial' test was hopeful of defeating New Zealand to gain the early advantage for the rest of the series.

New Zealand started badly in the match and was soon dismissed in its first innings for 81, a total that the

Englishmen later passed with only one wicket down. On the second day the MCC batsmen ran riot, flaying the New Zealand bowlers to all corners of the Carisbrook oval. J. H. Parks raised a century, W. Barber made 173, James Langridge 106 not out, Jim Human 97, Joe Hardstaff 76 and Holmes himself a whirlwind 54 not out in only 21 minutes.

The MCC score was 653 for 5 declared, giving them a lead of no fewer than 572 on the first innings!

In New Zealand's second innings absolute disaster seemed near as Ian Cromb, Gordon Weir and Jack Mills were soon out and New Zealand was reeling at 14 for 3 (in case you need reminding, that was still 558 runs behind!). However, there was a good recovery between 'Sonny' Moloney and Giff Vivian, which saw New Zealand through to 116 for 4 at stumps on the second day.

The third and final day dawned wet and miserable in Dunedin and all New Zealanders rejoiced at the prospect of securing a draw thanks to the obliging weather. Eventually that was the case, but only after one of the most bizarre spells of bowling seen in New Zealand cricket history — yet one that is listed in the record books simply as a maiden over. Confused? Read on.

Play on the third day began, but only after three o'clock in the afternoon. One of the overnight batsmen, Jack Lamason, was soon out and the English fieldsmen, with a weather eye on the black clouds overhead, obviously hoped to clean up the remaining wickets for an innings win before the storms returned. Play carried on in the murky weather. New Zealand lost a wicket here and a wicket there and their total limped along, still not a con-

sideration. The only imponderable was the weather. The MCC team eventually had the stubborn New Zealanders 7 down for 176. The outlook looked bad, concerning both the weather and the result.

It being assumed that Giff Vivian, approaching his century, would hold up the victory because he was handling the old ball with ease, the Englishmen adopted an outrageous plan to hasten the new ball into the attack.

Errol Holmes was off the field with a damaged hand, so the acting skipper, Jim Human, called for the ball. Standing by the umpire he proceeded to deliberately bowl wide after wide in an attempt to lift the score from 176 to 200 so that the new ball could be taken.

Vivian and Bill Meritt, the other batsman at the wicket, could only watch in wonder as the ancient game's laws were bent, extended and flouted by the club bearing the name of those who fashioned those very rules. In all, Human bowled an over of 24 assorted wides and byes and the 200 was reached. As wides and byes are not registered against the bowler's name, the official scorebook merely shows Human as having bowled a maiden over. Some over!

So the 200 came up for New Zealand. The new ball could be taken. The umpires (perhaps arm-weary from so much concerted signalling) handed over the new 'cherry' to Baxter, the MCC quickman, and back he went to his bowling mark to presumably come in and mop up the New Zealand tail and take out the match.

The small Dunedin crowd, stunned only minutes before at Human's inhumanity to cricket, were soon roaring with delight and satisfaction when,

Javed Miandad was a most popular Pakistan cricket captain in New Zealand in 1985. He was just as gracious in 1979. On the completion of a century at Lancaster Park he firstly shook hands with thirteen-year-old Stephen Ditfort of Xavier College, then posed *(right)* for the young man's camera. One is left wondering if Stephen's pic was a good one? *Photographs:* The Press, *Christchurch*

after only one delivery from Baxter to Vivian (on 87), the umpires upheld an appeal against the light and the players trooped from the field.

The match was, of course, a draw, but as all four tests in the series were draws Dunedin's weather could be thanked, for once, for sparing New Zealand a defeat that would have been hard to take because of the tactics adopted by the Englishmen.

Out . . . or Not Out?

From the 'You can't win' department. In 1952 during the cricket test at Eden Park between the West Indies and New Zealand, the Otago leg-spin bowler Alec Moir was bowling to Jeffrey Stollmeyer, the West Indian opening batsman. As one ball was hit into the field, the other opener, Alan Rae, who was backing up, slipped over when attempting to return to his batting crease. A New Zealand fielder underarmed the ball to Moir at the non-striking end and he could have easily broken the wickets to dismiss Rae who was still on the ground. Moir noted the West Indian's plight and proceeded to ignore the chance of lifting a bail for the run out. The grateful Rae, who was then on 9 not out, collected himself and went on to make 99 and share in a first-wicket partnership of 197.

Moir was criticised roundly from some quarters for not taking the outright chance to run out the man regardless of where he was. One paper at the time called Moir's act 'misplaced chivalry'. The incident made news all over the cricketing world.

In February 1978 at the second test between New Zealand and England at Lancaster Park there was a similar occurrence. Ewen Chatfield was the New Zealand bowler and Derek Randall was the non-striking batsman, backing up in much the same way as Alan Rae had been in 1952. As Chatfield ran in to bowl, he noticed Randall was out of his ground, backing up too soon. Chatfield stopped his delivery action and whipped the bails off and appealed. The umpire, Fred Goodall, had no option but to give the Englishman out.

Chatfield, too, was roundly criticised. His action was called 'a sad breach of the spirit of the game'.

Who was right in taking the action they did in those two test matches? Moir? Chatfield? The critics? My word, as I hear every season, cricket is a funny game!

Quick-quick-cricket

In these days of frantic one-day cricket action, wickets tumbling at the rate of 20 a day is a common occurrence. Another thing about one-day cricket is that a result is always achieved — provided of course it doesn't rain.

Consider, though, this game from the 1937 New Zealand cricket tour of the United Kingdom. Thirty-two wickets fell in one day on the way to an outright result. The difference is that this game, between New Zealand and Ireland in Dublin, was originally scheduled as a *three-day* first-class fixture.

Ireland batted first and made 79 all out. Their innings took 38 overs. New Zealand's batsmen in reply were no better at coping with the conditions. They were all out for 64 runs in 32 overs. In the afternoon Ireland batted again and lasted only 18 overs, making 30 all out. Jack Cowie, the big New Zealand fast bowler, took 6 wickets for 3 runs. New Zealand needed 46 to win and for once the pavilion-gate hinges got a little rest. Only 2 wickets fell in 10 overs and New Zealand scored the runs to win by 8 wickets.

The match, being originally a three-day game, was granted first-class status and was the first match of that quality in twenty-five years to be decided as an outright result in one day.

Perhaps, I hear you say, it could have happened only in Ireland! An Irishman might reply that it could only happen in a match involving New Zealand, now famed for the lowest ever test innings (26) and lowest ever test total (96)!

Rock Bottom at Eden Park

In years gone by New Zealand cricket followers have been a very patient breed. They have had to be. When the English cricket team arrived at Eden Park for the second test of 1955, those same fans were still waiting for New Zealand's first test victory. They had been waiting for twenty-five years. This was to be a watershed match for New Zealand cricket, but not in the way the Kiwis hoped. This was the day they hit rock bottom.

Surprisingly, a win for New Zealand in the match was a possibility at the end of both team's first innings. New Zealand had won the toss and captain Geoff Rabone had decided to bat. Bert Sutcliffe and John Reid, New Zealand's top two batsman, both got good scores, 49 and 73, facing an England bowling attack that included Frank Tyson, then bowling at his very fastest.

Rabone himself made 29 and New Zealand were all out for exactly 200. When England batted on the second day there were problems with the weather. Rain forced several breaks but on resumption New Zealand was soon looking good with England 164 for 7, still 36 behind. Tyson joined his captain, Len Hutton and they passed the 200 before the next wicket fell. Even when the last two English batsmen, Bob Appleyard and Brian Statham, helped add another 45 New Zealand was still considered to be in with a good chance of victory if it could get a big enough score in its second innings. For the pitch was considered to be likely to break up and favour the New Zealand spinners in the fourth innings of the match.

Sutcliffe and Gordon Leggat opened the New Zealand second innings only 46 runs behind on the first. Optimism was such that one cricket fan from Christchurch rushed to the airport to fly to Auckland to see the Kiwis win. By the time he arrived in Auckland, the game was over. England had won! Never was there seen such a procession of batsmen at Eden Park, or

indeed in any test match anywhere. Herewith is the New Zealand second innings scoreboard:

Leggat	*1*
Poore	*0*
Reid	*1*
Sutcliffe	*11*
McGregor	*1*
Cave	*5*
McGibbon	*0*
Colquhoun	*0*
Rabone	*7*
Hayes	*0*
Moir	*0 not out*
Extras	*0*
Total	*26*

It was a total score lower than the 30 runs South Africa had twice been dismissed for in their test history. The New Zealand innings lasted 104 minutes and 27 overs and there was only one boundary hit. One waggish Canterbury writer reminded his readers that the four Canterbury players in the New Zealand team had travelled nearly 5000 miles in total for the match and between them had scored 1 run in the second innings.

Let me quote from *Memorable Moments of New Zealand Sport*:

The 13,500 spectators at Eden Park, who for two-and-a-half days had watched an enthralling, low-scoring struggle, sat stunned. They had seen New Zealand batsmen fail before and had been able to mix cheers with jeers.

But this murderous procession was too much. They sat silent, numbed, uncomprehending — the only sounds being the ball hitting the stumps, the typewriters tapping at the left-hand end of the old number 1 stand and the steady creak of the hinges

The great Gary Sobers, batting attractively as usual. But, for all his great achievements in the cricketing game, his form against New Zealand was — surprisingly — only modest.

on the players' gate in front of the members' stand.

When that grey afternoon was all over, they stood and shuffled out, carrying with them their embarrassed hush. They had seen the lowest innings scored in a test match. They had suffered much for New Zealand cricket in the past — but this was the ultimate humiliation.

Sobering Thoughts

Down the years New Zealand has been lucky enough to see most of the world's top cricketers in action. Walter Hammond once made consecutive test innings in New Zealand of 227 and 336 not out. Everton Weekes, in the fifties, made five consecutive centuries on a West Indian tour. The Chappell brothers, Ian and Greg, each made two hundreds at Wellington in 1974 while names like Hutton, Walters, Cowdrey,

May, McGlew, Compton, Worrell, Walcott, Hanif and many other top-liners have all been seen to advantage by Kiwi cricket fans. However, a big disappointment was the fact that throughout his long career Sir Donald Bradman never once could be enticed to make the short journey across the Tasman seas to play on our wickets.

But one of the other very great names in world cricketing history did play in New Zealand on two tours. Though he plundered bowlers for many big scores all over the world and took many a wicket or fine catch, the great West Indian Sir Garfield Sobers never really 'came off' against New Zealand teams.

No adequate reason can be advanced for his repeated failures with the bat and ball in New Zealand except to say that on his second tour here (in 1969), he may have been battle-worn from the cricketing pressures in Australia.

Sobers had 16 first-class innings in his two tours of New Zealand and only twice did he pass 50 runs; a 53 against Canterbury was his best against a full provincial or test team. (He did also score 54 in a special Sir Frank Worrell Memorial match in Auckland in 1969.) On other occasions in New Zealand he positively dithered about. In the fourth test at Auckland in 1956 he could make only 1 and 1 in the match. He made two ducks in 5 test innings in 1968–9.

With the ball the story is not much different. His 13 first-class wickets in New Zealand cost him over 40 runs each, extraordinary when you consider he was a fine left-arm bowler and in all honesty, some of the New Zealand provincial teams, and indeed test teams, were not of the greatest standard.

It should be added that figures do not always tell the true story. I well recall Sobers's innings of 39 in the test at Wellington in 1969. It was a cameo of all that is great in the art of batsmanship. Superb shots flowed all about the field and the man soon reached 39 runs, only to feed a catch to Victor Pollard and be on his way. Many of his other innings in New Zealand were equally as graceful but ended too soon to be rated as great knocks.

With his paltry average against Kiwi bowlers in mind, the New Zealand touring cricket team visited the West Indies in 1972 and came up against Sobers on his home pitches. It was not really very much different. In the first test he managed a 13 not out, then followed a 19 and 9 in the second. It was only in the third test at his home town in Barbados that Sobers really flourished against Kiwi bowling. He made 35 in the first innings, another modest effort before coming in at number 7 in the second innings batting order. Joining Charlie Davis with the West Indies still 120 runs from an innings defeat with only 5 wickets left, Sobers finally unleashed his full batting array. He made 142 in the end and shared with Davis a sixth wicket stand of 254 which surely saved the test — and probably the series — for the West Indies.

In the fourth and fifth tests Sobers returned to 'normal' against New Zealand bowling, making scores of 5, 28 and 2 to give him an overall test average against New Zealand of 23.5, well below his career test average of over 57 runs per innings against all countries. Indeed, take out the score of 142 and the great West Indian's test batting average against New Zealand in 17 other innings was only 17!

Sutcliffe

The cricketing deeds of the legendary New Zealand left-hand batsman Bert Sutcliffe have been well recorded at a first-class level. In his career in top cricket, from 1941 to 1966, he hit bowlers of all descriptions for over 17,000 runs and averaged 47 per knock. He notched up 44 centuries, including 5 in test matches, and was known throughout the cricketing world as a fine stroke-maker, a gentleman and one of the game's greats.

Reading a back number of the old New Zealand monthly *The Sportsman*,

There was no finer prospect in New Zealand during the war years than the young Bert Sutcliffe. Come to think of it, he wasn't too bad after the war as well. Here is Sutcliffe in action in his first test series against England in 1947.

One of the most disappointing features of early New Zealand cricket was the fact that the great Don Bradman was never seen in action in this country. Yet he did come to New Zealand for a non-playing visit at the height of his career.

On the left, Bradman is pictured at Radio 2YA's microphone in September of 1932. He visited the Wellington radio station during a stopover by the Australian team on their way home from a tour to the United States. Bradman gave an interview while his teammates played an exhibition match at the nearby Basin Reserve Ground!

The second visit the great 'Don' made was in 1971. Then knighted, Sir Donald is pictured below giving an interview to the author in Auckland.

Incidentally, Don Bradman played against a New Zealand team once: that was in Adelaide in 1937. He played for the South Australian State side and was out for only 11. He was caught by wicketkeeper Eric Tindall, bowled by Jack Cowie. Both the New Zealanders involved were outstanding sportsmen of their day.

I see that Sutcliffe's record before he came into first-class cricket was as impressive reading as his later test record. For instance, he is one of Takapuna Grammar's most accomplished old boys. While he was at that school he played in only one cricket team — the first XI. As a fourteen-year-old in his first year he easily found first XI cricket within his powers and the schoolmasters responsible never saw any reason to change his place in that team. By his third year (of five) he was captain leading much older boys in the team.

The records of Bert Sutcliffe at Takapuna Grammar must have been meticulously kept. *The Sportsman* says his average for his five years in the first eleven was 71.8. In all he made 2730 runs for his school and his best score was a 268 plundered off an unnamed Auckland rival college. The young Sutcliffe was so good in his last year that he averaged 149 runs per innings over the whole season.

In light of these achievements it is little wonder that 'Sutty' was put straight into the Auckland Brabin Cup team, a selection of the city's most promising players. In his first two innings Bert knocked up 119 against Canterbury and 108 against the Taranaki Colts. He played his first match for Auckland the following season, allowing himself a comparative failure on his debut. (He made 11.)

At the age of twenty-one, towards the end of the war Sutcliffe was included in the Second New Zealand Expeditionary Force which journeyed to North Africa. There, cricket was well organised for the troops and Sutcliffe soon found himself in the big leagues. In his first match, for Digla

against Helwan, he cracked a score of 73. Then in a vital match (vital for the morale of the New Zealand soldiers) he thumped the South African corps bowlers for 159 not out in only 170 minutes. It was a record score for any player on the Alamein ground. Sutcliffe beat that record with a masterly 163 a few weeks later.

All this high scoring made him an obvious choice for the British Empire Forces XI who played the United Kingdom team. Sutcliffe and ex-New Zealand player Jack Lamason made nearly 100 between them (Sutcliffe 34) and the Empire beat the UK, a result that was warmly received by all the Kiwis so far from home.

None of those who saw the young Sutcliffe, either at college in Auckland or in the heat of the desert, were surprised when on his return to civilian life, he went on to become one of New Zealand's greatest cricket players.

Trumper's Conquerors

In 1913 a wealthy New Zealand businessman, Arthur Sims, sponsored a tour of New Zealand by leading Australian players. The tour was not officially approved by the Australian Board of Control but most of the leading Australian cricketers of the day responded to the chance of a visit to New Zealand.

The Australian team was, in the end, a very strong one, too much so for their Kiwi opposition. In sixteen matches in New Zealand they totalled 6762 runs with some huge averages and quite incredible scoring. This is how some of the scores read: 658, 461, 563, 354, 709, 510, 610/6 and — the

daddy of them all — 922 for 9 against hapless South Canterbury at Temuka! In the Australian team there were such illustrious giants of the game as Victor Trumper, 20-stone Warwick Armstrong, Monty Noble, Herbie Collins and Arthur Mailey.

Poor South Canterbury! Although the Australians batted for only 330 minutes against them, they flayed the local bowling mercilessly. Jack Crawford made 354, including 14 sixes and 45 fours. Others down the scorebook read Trumper 135, L. Cody 106, Noble 77 not out, W. McGregor 74, Vernon Ransford 57. The partnership between Trumper and Crawford added 293 for the eighth wicket in 69 minutes, and they took the total from 450 to 550 in only 23 minutes! South Canterbury, it must also be admitted, were allowed a fifteen-man team for the match! One of their bowlers, Rix by name, conceded bowling figures of 5 for 226. South Canterbury, in their only innings, made 180.

The Australian innings was a world record for most runs scored by any team in one day. While it was a momentous achievement for them, it remains to this day one of the lesser days of reward for South Canterbury cricket!

Question: *Which was the first New Zealand cricket team to go through England on a full tour and not lose a game?*

Answer: *The 1966 New Zealand women's team.*

Cycling

Many stories have come out of the sport of cycling in New Zealand. I am told on good authority that this next story happened in the way I have written it. I cannot reach the cyclist in question to check with him as he now lives in Canada. So my apologies if the story is not quite factually correct. As it is it's still well worth telling . . .

The Butter Dish

In the 1950s Max Grace of Auckland was a popular and determined cyclist in the regular events that made up each year's programme for that sport. The most prestigious, in road racing terms, was the Dulux 6 tour from Auckland to Wellington.

Here was a race that in a small way embodied the spirit of the great touring bike races of Europe. Each year from 1960 a band of hardy cyclists and their backup crews would race all over the North Island, gradually heading further south towards the capital. In the cycling tradition there were prizes up for grabs on each day in the various stages of the race. In those days riders were strictly amateur. Money prizes were not permitted although, for pecuniary reasons, many riders did sell their winnings moments after receiving them.

Entered in the 1964 Dulux Race, the aforementioned Max Grace looked in the race-day programme as the race was headed from New Plymouth to Palmerston North via Wanganui and decided that of all the prizes listed for that day's ride the one he needed the most was the portable transistor radio that was to be presented to the winner of the sprint into the town of Bulls.

Grace took his place in the field and rode in the bunch for the earlier parts of that day's two stages. He conserved his energy but when the race approached Bulls, he moved up quietly through the other riders always with a view to bettering his position. He definitely had the winning of the transistor radio on his mind.

The town sprint in Bulls took place near a bridge just past the town and when he saw the flag ahead signalling the sprint's finish Max Grace launched himself into a huge burst of spped. He left the others behind and dashed across the line to take the plaudits of the waiting crowd. Feeling satisfied at achieving his goal, he then sat back in the bunch for the rest of the way, possibly dreaming of all the fine music he would be able to enjoy on his new possession.

Imagine his chagrin when, at the stage prize presentation later in the day, he was called forward to receive the handsome trophy but was instead presented with a chrome-plated butter dish.

'But where's my tranny?' Grace is reported to have asked, somewhat testily. When it was pointed out to him that he had apparently misread the prize schedule and that the transistor radio was, in fact, the reward for the next sprint after Bulls, Grace gazed ruefully at his new unwanted, unneeded prize. All that effort for a bloody butter dish!

The incident, it seems, bothered Max Grace. Certainly he carried on in the race and did well, too, picking up his share of other prizes along the way. But never a transistor radio.

After the race's conclusion a few of the Auckland riders, including Grace, packed all their gear and winnings into a vehicle and set out on the long haul back to their home town.

As they were heading north, Max Grace made a special request of the vehicle's driver. 'Could you please,' he asked, 'make a quick stop for me at Bulls? There's something I've got to do.'

Approaching the town Grace directed the driver towards the bridge where he had had such high hopes in the sprint finish only days previously. There the vehicle was parked.

Max Grace then climbed from his seat, rummaged through his belongings until the butter dish prize for the sprint into Bulls came into his hands.

He then stood up, walked to the edge of the bridge and with great solemnity he flung the dish, with all his strength, out across the river. It hit the water and sank slowly out of sight.

Grace waited at the bridge until he could no longer see the dish. Satisfied at last, he returned to the vehicle, climbed in, settled down in his place and peacefully rode the rest of the way home.

Splash!

The 1986 Chartwell Tour of the Waikato province was one of the bigger events of the cycling year. It was keenly contested and won in the end by Thomas Wegmueller of Switzerland.

The highlight of the ride, so they tell me, was not one of the sprints or one of the hill climbs but instead the actions of a rider named Paul Rogers, one of the new breed of New Zealand cyclists.

Rogers was racing somewhere behind the leaders on a stage in the French Pass area of Waikato. At one point he and another rider found themselves on a steep, speedy descent.

The slope was such that they were able to make great haste and the two riders soon caught up with a van that was also travelling on the same road. The van picked up speed to keep ahead of the riders and soon they were all zipping downhill at over 80 kilometres per hour.

When I say that the two riders were behind the van I do not mean to suggest they were cheating in any way. But their closeness to the van meant that they had no way of seeing the twists and turns of the road ahead. They just followed the line of the van. And hoped. So when the van reached the bottom of the hill and made a sharp right turn on to a bridge the cyclists had no knowledge of the change of direction that was needed.

Paul Rogers missed the turn and ploughed off the road. Unfortunately for him he departed right at the edge of the bridge. There was a neat gap and through it Rogers and his bike journeyed at top clip. The man and the bike literally took off into nothingness. They flew through the air and landed with a mighty splash in the mighty Waikato River.

The story can be told in a light-hearted vein as Rogers suffered no injury apart from a bruising of the ego for such an undignified exit from the race.

My source for this story tells me the funniest part of the whole episode may have been the look on the St John's medical officer's face when they were radioed to turn back and 'fish out' the rider who had crashed out of the race by the French Pass Bridge!

Doing Well

In his younger days, Radio New Zealand's cycling reporter, John Cardwell, was a prominent bike rider in Auckland with a youthful burning ambition to ride in the Dulux Six-Day Race from Auckland to Wellington.

His best chance came in 1977 when he sent his entry and trained assiduously for the long ride. However, bad luck was to dog his hopes. Several weeks before the race he received confirmation of his entry and received a number to wear, number 15. But then an Achilles' heel injury struck and a hugely disappointed Cardwell had to send back his number and withdraw from the race.

The race organisers realised they would have a gap in the race programme, which had already been printed and which contained John Cardwell's name next to the number 15. The same officials were therefore more than relieved when the very talented Auckland youngster Roger Sumich, who had just returned from riding in Europe, made a late entry.

With the race field full, Sumich was given Cardwell's entry and number. However, it was too late to change the published details in the race programme.

Imagine Cardwell's subsequent surprise and amusement when Sumich had considerable success in the race while all the while the local newspaper reporter travelling on the tour kept referring to number 15 as 'J. Cardwell of Auckland'.

While significant sprints, stages and hill climbs drew reference to 'Cardwell' doing well it was the young Sumich who was being done out of recognition and publicity.

To this day, John Cardwell retains the clippings made by that particular reporter. They come in handy when people approach him and ask, 'What do you know about a six-day bike race? You never rode in one, did you?'

If at First You Don't Succeed . . .

The top sportsman's career normally charts a familiar pattern: early promise is followed by rising success which culminates in a pinnacle of achievement; after that comes the downhill slope as age takes its relentless toll, and finally retirement or a movement into management. However, for Wellington's Neil Lyster, an Olympic and Commonwealth Games representative in the sport of cycling, there was no such 'normal' career.

In 1968, as a twenty-year-old, the brilliant youngster won his way into the New Zealand cycling team for the Mexico Olympic Games. Lyster went, marched in the opening ceremony and enjoyed all the thrills that come from being part of the greatest of all sporting festivals. *Except for one thing.* At the Games Lyster was reduced to fixing the other riders' bikes as he waited out a selectorial choice that favoured his team mates. He did not ride in a single event, being officially the reserve for the road and time trial teams.

Stung by what he thought was a wrong selection, Lyster embarked on a long build-up to the next major cycling excursion — the Commonwealth Games in Edinburgh in 1970. Again the path for Lyster was not easy. Finishing second in two of the New Zealand trials for those games, third in another event and fourth in two others, Lyster found himself not strong enough in any one event to be finally selected. His only satisfaction was that he was nominated to travel by the cycling selectors, but this was not endorsed at Commonwealth Games selection level.

By 1972 and the Munich Olympics Lyster had changed his emphasis to

Neil Lyster, with that steely gaze of determination which won him countless New Zealand cycling championships on roads and tracks and which took him to the Olympic and Commonwealth Games many times.
Photograph: Dominion and Sunday Times

the Kiwi team finished fourteenth in the 4000-metre pursuit event.

Four years later New Zealand could not produce a pursuit team of even that quality and so the squad did not travel to the Montreal Olympics. By that year Neil Lyster was at the stage of his career where he was willing to try the management side of cycling. So Lyster, the reserve at Mexico and the competitor at Munich, marched at the Olympics for a third time, again in a different role. This time, at Montreal, he was cycling's section manager.

Next the story moves two years to the Commonwealth Games of 1978, also held in Canada, but in the bustling, oil-rich city of Edmonton in Alberta. By now Neil Lyster had changed again, and had made a successful returning-entry into national consideration as a track pursuit rider. His speed, strength and judgement of pace could not be ignored by the New Zealand selectors. He made the New Zealand 4000-metre squad and off to Canada he travelled once more. Further honours in Lyster's comeback came with his selection to carry New Zealand's flag in the opening ceremony.

Once competition began the New Zealand pursuit team quickly established itself as a medal prospect. Their ride in beating the powerful England team won the team of Kevin Blackwell, Jack Swart, Anthony Cuff and Lyster a gold medal chance in the final. But Australia's team had other ideas, and Neil Lyster and his three buddies had to settle for a silver medal.

No other Kiwi had gone Lyster's way, from being a reserve, omitted, then competing again to trying officialdom and then back to competing before he won a games medal.

pursuit riding. There was great delight when he made the team to travel to Germany, this time in an event where he would definitely compete. With his team mates John Dean, Paul Brydon and Blair Stockwell, Lyster gave Olympic competition all he had. But success did not come at those games —

HOCKEY

Worth the Wait

One of the best stories of patience from the reserve bench concerns
Trevor Manning, the New Zealand hockey goalkeeper.

Manning was picked for the New Zealand Olympic hockey squad in 1968 and headed off with the others to Mexico City. There he sat out the opening game against India for which Ross McPherson of Northland was the New Zealand keeper. When New Zealand won that game and the whole country rejoiced at the defeat of the Tokyo gold medallists, great hopes were held for a medal for New Zealand. The selection policy of the team involved keeping the same combination so poor Manning watched from the sideline and sat out every game of that Olympic competition.

Came the Munich Games of 1972 and Trevor Manning was still around and one of the top hockey goalkeepers in the country. Again he and McPherson were chosen to travel with the New Zealand hockey squad to the Olympics. As at Mexico, Manning was soon relegated to the reserves (or 'emergencies' as New Zealanders used to call them).

Those sad Games finished and in the hockey New Zealand dropped two places from the seventh place it had occupied four years before. But still there was no place for the Wellingtonian Manning in any game. The bald facts were that he had been twice to the Olympic Games and had not been called on once to play.

But every dog has his day. Came 1976 and Ross McPherson's long reign as the number one goalkeeper had passed into hockey history. McPherson had been a very worthy New Zealand representative.

New Zealand was nowhere near the favourites before the Montreal hockey contest. However, by consistency and steadiness they won their way through to the final with Manning this time firmly ensconced as number-one goalkeeper. His long wait to play Olympic hockey became the ultimate satisfaction when New Zealand won the final against Australia. Yet the moment of victory was for Trevor Manning very sweet and very painful.

New Zealand led 1–0 into the last ten minutes of the final. The desperate Aussies fired ball after ball at the New Zealand goal. Time after time the Kiwis were saved by Manning, the hero. However, one shot was hit so sharply at the Kiwi goal that it smashed Manning's knee even though he was, of course, wearing massive padding.

When the moment of victory and exhaltation came Trevor Manning cheered through teeth clenched with pain. But the long wait to play Olympic hockey had been well worthwhile.

Netball

England Rules OK?

In 1938 netball was a thriving 9-aside game, then known as basket-ball, among the young women of New Zealand, yet when in that year a national squad was first selected — for a tour of Australia — the team ended up playing 7-aside!

This is how netballers used to look in the traditional pose 'Outdoor Basketball' teams took in the old days. Here is the Auckland team of 1940, winners of the New Zealand Centennial Tournament.

This extraordinary situation arose because Australia and New Zealand espoused rather different sets of rules. A compromise was reached whereby any points that could not be agreed upon should be settled by reference to English rules. And since the English played 7-aside, the New Zealanders found themselves playing an unfamiliar game in their first test matches. Not surprisingly, the Aussies won the series, and another in 1948, and New Zealand officially adopted the 7-aside game only in 1959.

Be that as it may, the Kiwi women have a record at the world championships that is second to none:

1963	*Runners-up in England*
1967	*Winners in Perth, Australia*
1971	*Runners-up in Kingston, Jamaica*
1975	*Third place in Auckland, New Zealand*
1979	*First equal in a three-way tie with Australia and Trinidad-Tobago in Port of Spain, Trinidad*
1983	*Runners-up in Singapore*
1987	*Winners in Glasgow, Scotland*
1991	*Runners-up in Sydney, Australia*

The best scores that the New Zealand team have ever put up were the 117–9 win over Singapore in 1974 and a

The greatest moment in the history of New Zealand netball. At Perth in 1967, Judy Blair of Canterbury leads her New Zealand team under the victory arches of the flags of the other competing teams at the world championships. No other New Zealand team has done better than that.

The New Zealand netballers have played in some strange places. Here they are in a warm-up game in Jamaica before the 1963 world championships. They won this game too. *Photograph:* Daily Gleaner, *Jamaica*

112–4 thumping of Northern Ireland in 1963.

The oddest thing about these results is the fact that their worst performance — third — came when they were playing at home. Who says it's an advantage to be host nation?

Racing

Cardigan Bay's Last Run

Among the most loved of all New Zealand's sporting heroes is the horse Cardigan Bay. This pacer, owned by Mrs Audrey Dean of Auckland, won eighty races in a long and distinguished career that took it to fame and fortune in New Zealand, Australia and the United States. Under the expert handling of reinsman Stanley Dancer, Cardigan Bay became the first pacer to win one million dollars in stake earnings.

The public admiration for this horse was unparalleled in the harness-racing game. So when his career was over and he returned to retire in New Zealand, it was decided that the great horse should give a final solo exhibition of his genius on Auckland's 'Ribbon of Light' track at Alexandra Park. A huge crowd turned out to bid him farewell and great was the excitement as the champion paced at great speed down the back straight and headed for the home stretch.

Media interest in the farewell to Cardigan Bay had been high and all of Auckland's leading racing writers and commentators were in position to record his last run. In those days television was in its infancy in this country, but there was enough far-sighted thinking around to ensure that a film crew was dispatched to the track to record this finale for the pacing fans in other parts of the country, and indeed for posterity.

The cameraman, who has since died but who should perhaps, in the light of events, remain nameless, positioned himself above the straight in a perfect viewing-place to see the great horse thunder again up the home straight. This was the track where, in years gone by, Cardigan Bay had won so many events, including the 1963 Auckland Trotting Cup when handicapped to start from 78 yards behind the barrier.

As Cardigan Bay, driven by his regular New Zealand driver Peter Wolfenden, ran to the corner of the track and headed for the finishing line, the television cameraman readied himself, eye at his viewfinder, finger on the start button of his camera. And when the great champion came into view he pressed his start button to go. The moment was as great as everyone had hoped it would be. 'Old Cardy' was in superb shape and even he seemed to feel the occasion and understand the great roar of admiration given by 30,000 throats as he thundered down the straight, passing the finishing post to run on into retirement. A lovely way to end a great career.

And what of the TV film? Unless there were amateurs in the crowd filming, there is no record of this historic moment. Television's cameraman had rolled his camera all right, and he had followed the horse perfectly in his viewfinder all the way to the finish line, but only one thing had he forgotten and that was to put some film in the camera!

Cardigan Bay never raced again.

Question: *When the great old New Zealand-bred horse Carbine won the Melbourne Cup in 1890, how many horses were there in the field?*

Answer: *Thirty-nine!*

Moifaa

In the late nineteenth century a Mr A. Allingham of Hawke's Bay bred a horse which was named Moifaa. It became a chaser and was good enough in 1901 to win the Great Northern Steeplechase at Ellerslie in Auckland, then as prestigious a win as it is today.

Moifaa was then purchased by another Hawke's Bay racing enthusiast who sent the horse to England to try for some of the rich jumping prizes available there.

Transporting a horse to a faraway place was not the relatively comfortable operation that it is in today's jet age. The ship that transported Moifaa ran into difficulties off the coast of England, and was totally shipwrecked in a wild storm. Brave Moifaa, so the story goes, leapt into the sea and swam ashore. After recovering from this harrowing ordeal and being taken to his proper destination, the horse resumed his training.

In 1904 Moifaa started in the Liverpool Grand National, so named then but later to be known as the Grand National, and ran on the Aintree course. Moifaa won that race, beating King Edward VlI's horse, Ambush II. Edward, sensing he had seen a champion in action, immediately set out to buy the New Zealander for his own stable. The kingly sum of 2000 guineas changed hands and Moifaa became royal property.

From all accounts the horse, with its brave background of survival and courage, became the King's firm favourite. In 1905 he ran in the Liverpool Grand National wearing Edward's colours, but could only man-

age second for the King in the race he had won for New Zealand the year before.

The King, however, never reduced his affection for Moifaa. It became the mount for him at all ceremonial occasions from then on. And at the King's funeral on 6 May 1910, the shocked populace (he had been ill only three days) saw the cortège pass with two animals near the front of the procession. One was the King's favourite dog, his white-haired terrier named Caesar. And the other animal was the New Zealand horse that swam for his life, Moifaa.

Not-so-immaculate Conception

In the world of horses New Zealanders pride themselves on the quality of their breeding industry, both thoroughbred and standardbred. Not always, though, have bloodlines been what they have been made out to be . . .

Just after the Second World War, when the sport of trotting was resuming, there were a few wags around the Hutt Park track near Wellington. Don Nyhan, the sucessful Templeton trainer, remembers the time when two brothers from Wainuiomata used to train a mare on the Hutt Park track. And each day the mare, called Cheetah, used to come past some stables where a number of stallions were quartered. On the days that she was in season, of course the stallions became more than a little agitated by her fleeting presence.

This regular upsetting of the stallions became irksome to the stablehands. Thus a couple of them (who shall remain nameless) plotted to release a stallion the next time Cheetah passed by in that delicate female condition.

Thus it came to pass that by a down-at-heel stallion, of no quality bloodline, the mare Cheetah became in foal. (The recounting of the tale does not accurately say where the mating took place, thank goodness!) Obviously there was acute embarrassment on all sides. But soon a handsome colt was born to Cheetah. And life went on . . .

The young horse grew up, was put into training and then was given the chance to race. In no time it proved to be a top-class trotter, sweeping all before it in race after race. Eventually the horse came to be accepted for a start in the highly prized New Zealand Trotting Cup, run at the famous Addington track in Christchurch. The horse of which I write duly stormed to the front of the classy field and raced home to win decisively the prestigious race. Everyone concerned was delighted. But the secret of his bloodline has been kept to this day.

The only hint that was ever given to the horse's irregular conception and vague paternity came in its name. Look up the winner of the 1946 New Zealand Trotting Cup and you'll be in on the joke too. The horse's name? Integrity, of course.

Integrity was unusual not merely in his conception. Despite his enormous talent and speed, in his early racing days he always — and inexplicably — got off to a slow start.

Doug Watts was his regular driver in those days and was meticulous about facing the horse to the right hand side for the start. It is a well-known fact that all trotters 'kick-off' from that side, facing the inside of the track to get a smooth beginning to their race-track running. Watts stuck to his task of making sure the horse was at least always in position at the barrier, facing right for the 'kickoff'. But his patience and preparation were never rewarded, and the horse became known as a bad starter.

One day at Addington, Integrity was being more than usually difficult as the field was being marshalled into line. Despite Doug Watts's efforts, Integrity ended up facing to the left and not the right. Then, before a manoeuvre could be made to turn him to the correct right hand side, the barrier dropped and the field was off.

Imagine then the surprise and delight of Watts when the horse kicked off beautifully and was away, in a twinkling, to a superb start.

Yes, you guessed it. It seems Integrity was a left-footed horse and nobody knew!

Rugby League

All Too Short

Ask a rugby league man to name the only Kiwi League team to be unbeaten on a tour of the United Kingdom and he'll be hard-pressed to answer. The reply is the 1939 New Zealand team.

The catch is that they played only two matches. The team left New Zealand by ship in August when the threat of Adolf Hitler's ambitions hung darkly over the whole world. They arrived in England a week before the outbreak of war and turned out for two matches, both of which they won. War was then declared and the New Zealanders returned home.

Some feel that that tour set back New Zealand rugby league for a number of years. The cost of sending a full squad by boat, in the financial climate of the times, was very high. Gaining little in the way of receipts from gate takings made the tour a major financial loss.

The New Zealand rugby league team fared marginally better than the Australian rugby union team which similarly arrived for a tour of the United Kingdom only days before war was declared. It played no matches at all.

Back home in New Zealand the Fijian rugby team was in the middle of its New Zealand tour when war was declared. In fact, twenty-four hours after the fateful day a crowd of 17,000 went to Eden Park to see Fiji beat Auckland 17–11. Rugby authorities allowed the tour to be completed and it continued for a further fortnight. The Fijians went through the tour unbeaten, still the only country to do so on a full rugby tour of New Zealand.

Catastrophe at Carlaw Park

Auckland's Carlaw Park has not always presented itself in the best of condition for the playing of the game of rugby league, but in its time it has produced many memorable days for New Zealand sport. Doreen Lumley equalled a world sprint record on its surface, George Best and Bobby Charlton led Manchester United to a big soccer win over Auckland there, and many have been the days when boxers and league players have won glory in their respective sports.

But one day in 1963 Carlaw Park witnessed a game that every Kiwi present will want to forget. That was the day New Zealand's rugby reague team played South Africa.

Rugby league had not truly established itself in South Africa. Their team was instead mostly made up from those who had changed from rugby union and gone to play in England. Others were domestic South African players who were disgruntled about the amateur game and wanted to cash in on their sporting ability. A South African rugby league was formed and there were hopes that the game would be as popular there as it was in Australia, New Zealand, France and Great Britain. But there were only six clubs formed in the South African League and therefore their national team was chosen from only about eighty players.

There were further difficulties when some English clubs would not release their South African players for the tour. Thus the 1956 rugby union stars Wilf Rosenberg and Tom van Vollenhoven and the 1960 Springbok Hennie van Zyl were not available.

In the Australian section of the tour the South African rugby league team took a true hammering. They were first given two games 'in the bush' which they won comfortably, but once the tourists came to the cities of

Sydney and Brisbane, the home of league in Australia, they never won another match! The team took some fearful hidings and Sydney beat them 49–5, Queensland beat them 32–16 and Australia won the two internationals 34–6 and 54–21. Even the Parramatta Club team from Sydney beat South Africa by 39 to 18!

When the Springboks came to New Zealand for four games at the end of their tour, they were a sorry sight. Not only was their morale at rock bottom, but injuries had severely depleted their lineup. Indeed there was serious thought of abandoning the New Zealand part of the tour and calling the whole operation quits with just the Australian defeats to reflect on. More big scores were predicted against the tourists, in particular once they reached Auckland.

The South Africans opened their New Zealand tour with a game against Wellington at the Basin Reserve. Included in the touring team were men like Dawie Ackermann, Martin Pelser and Natie Rens who had played against the All Blacks in years gone by. In the team were four others who had played for their country at the fifteen-aside game.

South Africans had good reason to celebrate as they beat Wellington by 21 points to 12, though Wellington were no great shakes at league and had never beaten a touring team. But results for the South Africans returned to normal when they played against the South Island and Auckland. They lost both games and so went to the test as real underdogs.

New Zealand were buoyant at the recent record of their test team. The year before they had beaten England

19–0 and 27–8 so they were odds-on to thrash the South Africans.

The tourists' woes were compounded by further serious injuries. Their ranks had become so depleted that two Australian club players, Fred Anderson and Graham Wilson, had been invited to join the team just so that thirteen players could be fielded at each match in New Zealand.

So the South Africans arrived at Carlaw Park in August of 1963. The New Zealand team was dotted with the stars of the day — Mel Cooke, the Bailey brothers Roger and Gary, Bill Snowden, and the big Maori props Sam Edwards and H. K. ('Maunga') Emery. Altogether it was a strong side.

It was wet and cold and the Carlaw Park oval was at its notorious worst. The mud was clinging and cloying and the ball as slippery as soap. Slowly the tactics of the match emerged and it was South Africa who did better. Their rugby union backgrounds came to the fore as they used the slippery ground to telling effect. Time after time they sliced grubber kicks across the skiddy surface while the New Zealanders, who should have been more at home in the conditions, refused to use similar tactics.

The South Africans landed two penalty goals through their fullback Fred Griffiths, who had come to the team from a Sydney club side, but who was nevertheless a legitimate South African. To match that score the Kiwis tried attack after attack. Each time they were sent back by the Springboks' counter-kicks. A try by Gary Blackler, the hooker, was the best they could muster. As the darkness closed in and the mud became even thicker, the referee blew his whistle for full time. South Africa had won 4–3 in the biggest upset of New Zealand rugby league history!

While New Zealanders went away to consider how a team that had been hopelessly outclassed by even club sides had managed to beat their beloved Kiwis, the South Africans celebrated a win which their captain Ackermann said 'was really worth waiting for'.

Despite this famous victory, rugby league in South Africa failed to prosper, and indeed it wasn't long before it folded there completely. So that match on a wet, boggy Carlaw Park remains the only international league match played between New Zealand and South Africa.

Help!

The letter below was received by an Auckland radio station several years ago. It exemplifies a very direct desire by the writer to maintain an interest in a sporting event though the circumstances in which he lives are not conducive to such things.

Ref . . . Ref?

The Wellington rugby league referee Earl Pilcher of the late 1960s and early 1970s will have good cause to remember his day with the whistle at Carlaw Park when Auckland played Australia. Mr Pilcher was a top league referee in Wellington and always set a spectacular standard of neatness and tidiness before every match. His appointment to control the Auckland–Australia game was a tribute to his improvement as a referee, especially as the game in Wellington was then not as strong as league officials might have liked.

Dear Sir,

A number of us here are very keen on the Rugby League broadcasts you have planned for the next Kiwi tour.

We would appreciate it if you could forward to us the schedule of Broadcast times that you have recently been advertising on your station. Unfortunately it is not convenient for us to call and pick them up! Yours faithfully,

Rugby League Fan,
Mount Eden Prison, Auckland.

Ref! . . . Ref! . . .

Earl Pilcher's day at Carlaw Park came crashing down all about him when, during the course of the action, he accidentally collided with the big Australian forward Col Weiss. Down went Mr Pilcher to the ground while the game roared on — out of control if you like. The Auckland backs romped away for a try, which was scored by their fullback lan Young. As all the players stood about wondering when the whistle would sound for awarding of the score, Mr Pilcher was noted lying on the ground some distance away. He was out cold.

Naturally the try did not count and attention immediately centred on the poor referee. He was eventually carried from the field quite unable to continue, a sad end to his big day.

But the match had a happy ending for the Auckland fans. Even though the referee had been 'away with the fairies' when Young's try was scored, Auckland did not need it. They won 15–14 anyway, with the touch-judge Ron Caddy taking over the whistle for the rest of the game.

League meets Union

Auckland rugby league fans always like to remind those in the city who follow the sport of rugby union of the time when a team of league players won the prestigious Auckland rugby union's senior championship trophy. It sounds strange, indeed impossible that such a thing could have happened. But it did.

During the Second World War many of the traditional barriers in sport broke down. In those days in particular rugby league was much scorned by the administrators of the union game, but with so many young men being otherwise occupied, the two codes temporarily intermingled. League players were allowed into the union game, where they were welcomed with, shall we say, tentatively open arms.

Attention in Auckland centred on the Gallaher Shield competition, and in 1942 it was won by a pick-up team called Motor Transport Pool. MTP, as they were commonly called, played some great rugby on the way to the final, and then waltzed off with the trophy. Nothing surprising about that, you might think, except that the MTP team was composed almost entirely of league players. Their performance left league fans bursting with pride, and union followers bemused as to how it could have happened.

The Gallaher Shield is named after Dave Gallaher, captain of the 1905–6 All Blacks. In his life he resisted every temptation to transfer to the league game. Did he turn in his grave in 1942, I wonder, when a bunch of league men carried off 'his' trophy?

So Close

Over seventy years later, diehard rugby league supporters are still chortling over the action of the Canterbury rugby union in 1912.

At a meeting of the union that year a Mr S. F. Wilson suggested to those present that the breakaway game of Northern union (now known as rugby league) was in fact a better game than rugby union. Mr Wilson suggested that Canterbury adopt the new game and discard the old. He spoke with such persuasiveness and had such a following that the Canterbury meeting agreed to let the local rugby union clubs vote on the matter.

So they did at the next annual general meeting and the clubs supported the change from rugby union to Northern Union rules, but as an amateur game not professional.

The next step was to take the Canterbury plan to the New Zealand Rugby Football Union. There, with support from the unions of Auckland, Hawke's Bay, Bush, Canterbury, South Canterbury, Otago and Southland, the remit was put to the general vote. It lost 28–34. The Rugby union laws of the game stayed.

Those rugby union officials of today who have churlish attitudes towards the game of rugby league might do well to remember that but for six votes their own beloved game might have been an exact replica of that of their great rivals.

Rugby Union

All Black Days

In the history of New Zealand and its national game of rugby football there have been many glorious days.

On 3 September 1949 — the blackest day in New Zealand rugby history — these All Blacks in Durban played their test match knowing that another All Black team had been beaten hours before, back home.

Days like 1 September 1956 when, for the first time, New Zealand completed a test series win over their great rivals, the South African Springboks. Or like 29 November 1924, when the All Blacks scored one point for every year they had waited to avenge the infamous 1905 defeat by Wales. Or like 9 December 1978 when New Zealand beat Scotland to complete the first ever Grand Slam of wins by a New Zealand team on a tour of the four Home Nations. Or on 20 June 1987 when New Zealand beat France to win the first-ever World Cup.

Those days, and of course the many other days when we win, keep the sport of rugby firmly top of the pile as the national favourite of New Zealanders. But what of the days when things did not fare so well for the All Blacks?

Like 16 December 1905 when Wales upset the 'original' All Blacks by that 3–0 score. The controversial non-awarding of a try to the New Zealander Bob Deans lives on in the memory long after those who played in the game have passed on.

Or that dreadful 30 June 1928 when the All Blacks, full of hope, were thrashed 17–0 by South Africa in the first test of a series that the New Zealanders were later to square.

There were other days too when New Zealanders bit the bullet and inwardly burned with the distaste of defeat. It was a dark day on 25 September 1937 when South Africa clinched the test series with a 17–6 defeat at Eden Park. Then there was 21 December 1935 when Wales, by one 'lousy' point, beat New Zealand once again.

Discussions about which defeat and its ramifications caused the most distress among New Zealanders can be easily sorted out. If we assume that any test loss stings a good patriotic Kiwi to his absolute quick, then 3 September 1949 must take the prize. On that day the All Blacks lost not one but two rugby test matches. That unique if unpalatable occurrence came about through the generosity of the New Zealand Rugby Union in allowing New Zealand to play a home test series against Australia while the first-pick All Black team was in South Africa.

That All Black team on tour, under the captaincy of Fred Allen, had first call on players. They required thirty for the tour which meant that only the best of those remaining were available to play Australia. However, in 1949 it was still the policy of the day not to permit players with Maori blood to tour South Africa. Even if that was

wrong it did give the 'home' All Blacks three top Maori players to bolster their line-up. Ben Couch (latterly a Minister of Police and Maori Affairs), Johnny Smith and Vince Bevan were included in the All Black team for Wellington, and Smith was made captain. Australia were led by their brilliant centre three-quarter Trevor Allan and were unbeaten going into the test.

Some 32,000 people were at Athletic Park for the game and the Australians began the match in a much more assured fashion than did the New Zealanders. This was perhaps because the All Black team had been selected only twenty-four hours before playing! The Wallabies scored three tries in the first half, one of which was a fifty-yard dash for the line by the winger Ralph Garner, and the touring team led 11–0 at the changeover.

New Zealand managed a penalty goal to the fullback Jack Kelly, and late

Another day when things were hot for All Black rugby: 13 November 1978. Towards the end of the international between New Zealand and Wales, an All Black forward, Andy Haden, lept sideways out of a lineout in an attempt to persuade the referee he had been illegally pushed by a Welshman. The referee instead awarded a penalty to New Zealand and Brian McKechnie kicked a great pressure goal to win the game. Welsh people remember the first part as 'the lineout of shame', while New Zealanders refer to the winning kick as 'the goal of the century'.

in the match a try went to the winger Graham Moore. But Australia hung on to win 11–6 and the big crowd went home for a rest, one presumes, before getting up in the middle of the night to listen to Winston McCarthy's radio broadcast of the third test from South Africa.

Deep in the night the gloom did not lift from over New Zealand rugby. After only six minutes at Kingsmead Park, Durban, the Springboks were ahead by six points to nil, courtesy of two weird refereeing decisions and two penalties by their goal-kicking wonder, Aaron 'Okey' Geffin.

Like their brothers only hours before, the All Blacks in South Africa did not recover from the early scoring setback. Morrie Goddard, who had come in as centre (forcing the All Blacks to drop their captain, Allen), scored a try but a second-half penalty to South Africa, again goaled by Geffin, gave the Springboks a 9–3 winning score. The game was not a good one and for the second time in the series New Zealand had lost a test although the opposition had failed to score a try.

Sunday morning, 4 September, must have been something of a hangover time in New Zealand, recovering from two rugby defeats in the one day. But worse was to follow, as all rugby historians will recall. In the end, 1949 became easily New Zealand's worst as a rugby nation. The team in South Africa also failed to win the fourth test and so returned home as 4–0 series losers. Back home the 'other' All Blacks also fell to the Australians in the second test at Auckland. That meant six tests played in one season and all of them lost! An All Black year indeed!

Writing in the *Otago Daily Times* a local poet 'Clarence' summed up the year thus:

ALL BLACK BLUES — A TRAGEDY IN SIX TESTS

We'd better face the facts, you chaps,
And let the truth be understood;
So let us humbly doff our caps,
For we're no blooming good.
Since last July — forget it not —
We've played six tests — and lost the lot.

At Newlands last July, the tale
Was sad when Geffin found his mark;
Last week the final coffin nail
Was sunk on Eden Park,
Forgive if we our teardrops blink —
It's rather tragic — don't you think?

And blame the cooking, blame the chef,
The crowds (and don't forget the Press),
The wind, the weather, and the ref,
A biased linesman — Yes.
Such panaceas dim our woe
Just once or twice — but six times? No.

They say confession soothes the soul,
Then let us banish all the 'buts';
Let's own we lack the right control
And we can't play for nuts.
With our shortcomings thus confessed
Admit no flowers — by request.

Question: *Name the All Black who had the Christian name of Sanatorium?*

Answer: *Sana Torium Reid. The big Maori star of the All Blacks of the 1930s played on until 1949 when he toured Australia with the New Zealand Maori team.*

against Bay of Plenty as a prop. He last appeared for East Coast ten years before when he was a fullback.' Only an Arthur Carman could have kept tabs on such whims and fancies of rugby selection in such detail. And East Coast selection at that!

Incidentally, after his two games of first-class rugby — ten years apart and in two widely varied positions — Darling Moana was never heard of again (at least in the *New Zealand Rugby Almanack!*)

Almanack

The late Arthur Carman was a magnificent recorder of the facts and figures of New Zealand sport, from the 1920s to the late 1970s. Each year space was found on many a bookshelf throughout New Zealand for the annual editions of his rugby and cricket almanacks. They were 'musts' for the discerning Kiwi.

Carman had a most methodical approach to his task. Hardly a cricketing average was ever incorrect, no matter how 'small time' the batsman or bowler was; hardly a try was ever found missing or wrongly recorded. Arthur Carman was that type of man: thorough, exact, correct.

In his rugby almanacks I always admired the snippets of factual information with which he would fill a page when his other main texts had run out. These 'snippets' contained some gems of research and detail. I well recall the 1965 issue. At the bottom of one page was a four-line entry that summed up the Carman attention to who played where and how in New Zealand sport.

'Darling Moana', wrote Carman, 'appeared this year for East Coast

B-grade All Blacks

One of the most unusual rugby stories concerns the Wellington Football Club's rugby team in 1930.

The tale has its beginnings in 1929 when the club (don't ever call it the Wellington *Rugby* Club — they were originally a football club and so the name remains) played in the Senior A Champ-ionship. Although it had some excellent players within its ranks, a series of losses sent the team tumbling from Senior A status down to Senior 13.

This caused great sadness at the club as 1930 was its jubilee year. The celebrations looked as though they were going to be muted for a time, but as the 1930 season rolled around great loyalty to the Wellington Football Club's colours was revealed. The All Blacks Frank Kilby and Hugh McLean returned to the province from Wanganui and Taranaki where they had played the previous year. They joined Lance Johnson in the Wellington Club team as three who had played for their country. They were soon joined by the ex-Kaikorai and Otago winger Don Oliver and,

Although the wording on the ball says 'Senior' this Wellington Football Club team actually played Senior 'B' Grade. Included in their line-up are Hugh McLean (third from the left in the second row, standing), Don Oliver (second from left, sitting), Lance Johnson (third from left, sitting), Frank Kilby (fifth from left, sitting), and 'Rusty' Page (sitting on floor, extreme left). All were to become All Blacks.

freshly back from his spell at Sandhurst Military Academy, J. R. 'Rusty' Page, a brilliant five-eighths.

These five formed the basis of a team that was obviously going to be far too strong for Senior B play. In the first round of competition they won 79–0 and such was the high standard of their team play that they soon raced through the championship to win it easily. They thus won their way back into the Senior A at the first attempt, scoring in the process 495 points at an average of over 35 per match.

Furthermore, during that season Don Oliver was selected for the All Blacks against the British tourists, and the following season,1931, Rusty

Page also played for his country.

Though not strictly accurate, Wellington Club members have therefore claimed in the years since that their famous team of 1930 was the one that had five All Blacks in its ranks but was only good enough to be in Senior B.

Bricks

Although it happened in modern times, the sight of All Black backs practising with bricks surely made world history in Sydney in 1980.

It happened on the All Blacks tour after the team coach Eric Watson and

Ouch — it's the All Bricks

All Blacks centre Bruce Robertson takes the pass as winger Tim Twigden awaits his turn.

The All Blacks are tossing house bricks to each other to sharpen their game for tomorrow's third Test at the SCG.

Drastic cure for fumblers

All Blacks' coach Eric Watson left footballs on the sideline yesterday and moved to centrefield with three bricks.

So he sent his touring party on several lengths of the field passing the bricks along the line.

handling, so the All Blacks performed the way Watson hopes they'll handle the foot-

for something different, the news of this out-of-the-ordinary training method travelled fast. Soon there were TV crews and newspaper photographers in abundance recording this new training technique. One newspaper headlined their sports page 'Look out Australia — Here Come the All Bricks!'

And did the drastic cure for the fumblers work? That, I suppose, is in the eye of the beholder. But forty-eight hours later the All Blacks were hammered 26–10 by Australia.

This was the last time an All Back was sent off — except, of course, he didn't go. Alan Hosie of Scotland couldn't be more definite in his gesture in pointing Graeme Higginson towards the early shower when the All Blacks played Llanelli in 1980. Graham Mourie (*left*) later was part of a friendly group who decided with Mr Hosie that Higginson did not have to go off after all and that it was all just a misunderstanding. Hmmm . . . *Photograph by Peter Bush*

physiotherapist and trainer Malcolm Hood had decided that the players were not handling a leather rugby ball with enough certainty. The theory was that if the players took care with an object of much greater weight, then passing and catching a rugby ball in a match would be simplicity itself.

What followed was the unusual spectacle of New Zealand footballers, dressed in all their playing kit, passing builder's bricks from one to the other while carefully lapping the practice field.

In Sydney, where the media is so competitive and always on the lookout

SPORTSQUOTE

Censored!

'I'll never play another game like that, I'm absolutely buggered.' With these words in a live radio interview after the fourth test of 1956 against the Springboks, All Black Peter Jones set off a furore. It was a major talking-point, and many papers quoted the interview with the offending word

THE KNOCKOUT

Called to address the crowd at Eden Park today after the Test in which he had played so magnificently, Peter Jones, the North Auckland forward, made the biggest hit of the afternoon. "Ladies and gentlemen," he said, "I hope I don't have to play in such a tough game again. I am absolutely b———." Don Clarke confined his remarks to "Thank you."

One of the author's prized possessions. A picture of the incident at Eden Park in 1956, autographed in typically colourful fashion by Peter Jones. The cutting shows how one newspaper of the time told its readers of the dreaded 'word' used by 'Tiger' Jones.

coyly printed as 'b.........'. For a long time radio refused a replay, though it has been broadcast in more recent and liberal times.

Question: Much was made in 1983 of the fact that the Wairarapa-Bush Rugby prop Bill Rowlands achieved the feat of playing against four different British Isles Rugby teams. The frequency of All Black tours to the northern hemisphere means it has been possible for British players to play against a much higher number of New Zealand teams than our players could against overseas touring teams to New Zealand. For instance, in how many different years did Andy Irvine play against All Black teams in Europe?

Answer: Andy Irvine played against the All Blacks in Europe in five different years. In 1973 (for Scotland in Scotland); 1974 (for the Barbarians at Twickenham); 1978 (for Scotland and the Barbarians); 1979 (for Scotland); and 1981 (for the French Barbarians in Bayonne).

Champagne Rugby

Almost all international sporting events are played to their completion in the most serious of atmospheres and circumstances. As the old cliché says — no quarter is asked for and none is usually given. But the 1976 All Blacks, on their way home from a long tour of Argentina, played a game that was completely different from all those hundreds of other stern encounters down the years.

The New Zealand team under Graham Mourie agreed to play a friendly match against the former French fullback Pierre Villepreux's Tahiti fifteen. Rugby on that friendly isle is not a stern test for an international team (quite the opposite in fact), so the crafty locals tried other means to upset the New Zealanders.

Instead of having the party for the game afterwards — as is a rugby tradition — the Tahitians had it beforehand! And they were very heavy on the hand with the French champagne! The All Blacks, according to my impeccable source, went on to the field several hours later well at the disadvantage of several vintage bottles of bubbly.

This made for a lively game played, my man tells me, in mock seriousness and much humour in front of a crowd of 10,000.

Unfortunately for the locals their mischievous plan to beat the mighty All Blacks rebounded on to themselves. Many of the home team also suffered from rather too much pre-game imbibing. The score therefore crept up at regular intervals. Forty points were passed by the All Blacks in their gay mood. Then 50, 60, 70 and more.

Eventually the New Zealanders tried tactics designed to slow their own game down, both for their delicate states and out of consideration for their generous hosts. The All Blacks swapped forwards for backs and tried the game that way. Big Andy Haden found himself at halfback. Impish Kevin Green took Haden's place in the forwards. But still the points came.

At the end, I am told on good authority, 82 points had been scored by New Zealand to a mere 9 by Tahiti. Manawatu's Ken Granger scored 5

tries and Stu Wilson 4. The odd thing is that not one of the All Blacks who played in the game (that I have managed to speak with) can recall exactly how the game ended. All most can say is, 'What a day!' when asked to speak in detail about this match-to-end-all-matches.

Perhaps it was because the after-match function was held beforehand that this match was not given first-class status. Everyone knows such activities are against International Rugby Board rules!

Question: *Name the All Black of the 1970s who ended his All Black days by playing his last four games in four different forward positions?*

Answer: *Bob Barber of Southland on the All Black tour of Australia and Fiji in 1974. His last four games were against Australian Capital Territory (as Number 8 forward), Queensland (as a flanker), Queensland Country (as a lock) and Fiji (as a prop).*

Eton

The 1924 All Black Alf West from Taranaki was such a 'hard case' that not even his team mates could work him out. Born in Inglewood, he played his rugby for Hawera. He was a tough customer — 'one of the hardest forwards to play for New Zealand' said Winston McCarthy in his book *Haka — The All Blacks Story*.

As I said, not everyone found West to their liking. From that tour of 1924 comes this lovely snatch of conversation:

'That chap West. He obviously wasn't brought up at Eton.'

'No mate, he was eaten and then brought up!'

Cricket or Rugby?

When the 1974 All Black team beat South Australia by 117 points to 6, the news of the game was greeted with much scorn in the newspapers of the Australian Rules-mad city of Adelaide. One newspaper headlined its story: 'New Zealand All Blacks 117–6. South Australia bats tomorrow!'

SPORTSQUOTE

Good and Bad Losers

The 1970 All Blacks returned from South Africa on the wrong end of a 3–1 test scoreline, but their manager, Ron Burke, still managed a philosophical comment: 'Even though we lost the test matches, the tour was still a success.'

Less happy was the manager of the 1983 British Lions tour to New Zealand; Willie John McBride's most (in)famous comment was: 'We didn't come here to be intimidated.'

Haka

The 1978 All Blacks came through an extremely tough tour of the United Kingdom with much success. They lost only one game out of eighteen, their single defeat being the 'infamous' one (to them, at any rate!) at the hands of Munster. All of the remaining tour matches were played in a deadly serious state of mind, though there was

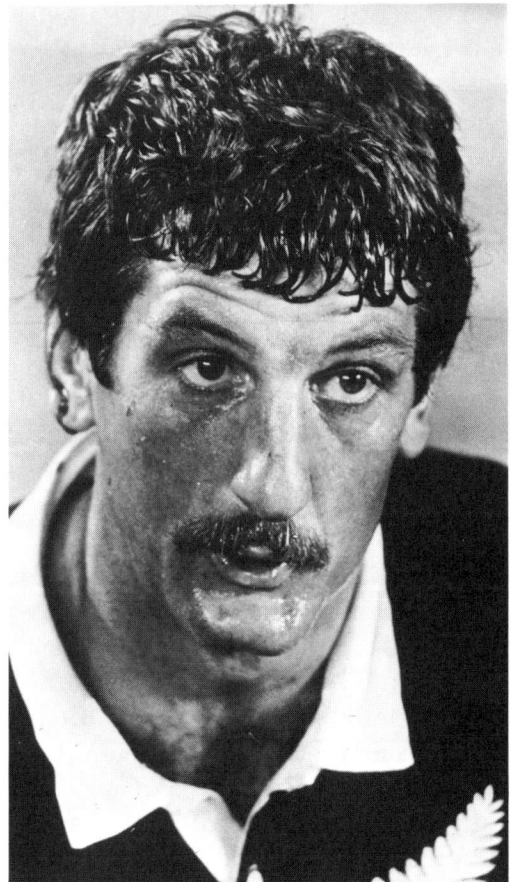

Graham Mourie, the great All Black captain. But his ploy designed to distract the Barbarians team in 1978 was definitely not his greatest tactical plan!
Photograph by Peter Bush

sometimes the odd incident of rough play to tickle the twitching typewriter fingers of the sensational element of the Fleet Street rugby writers.

As the tour approached its conclusion New Zealand's outstanding captain, Graham Mourie, obviously felt that some levity was required to counter all the dreadful seriousness that lately had flooded the front pages of the daily papers. An incident in the second-to-last tour game at Bridgend involving the New Zealander John Ashworth and the Welshman John Williams had caused some graphically sordid front-page stories.

So Mourie proposed that at some point during the last tour game, against the famous Barbarians Club to be played at Cardiff Arms Park, he would give a secret signal to his team and they, being good Kiwis, would begin, in the middle of the playing time of the game, a traditional Maori haka.

Such a diversionary tactic, Mourie schemed, would maybe produce a smile or two and make a welcome change from what had been seen in the newspapers or on television over the course of the previous four days. If the opposition was also diverted from the rugby action perhaps startled by the sight of grown rugby players doing a crazy war-dance, Mourie could see in his mind his team galloping away for a brilliantly conceived and hilarious try.

Soon the big day rolled around and the All Black players were all well schooled to act immediately on Mourie's call when it came. Imagine the scene. Cardiff Arms Park, pulsating to the roar of 50,000 excited fans

Isn't it great when a game like rugby union can create such friendship and cameraderie between its greatest players? Here two of the all-time greats Bryan Williams (left) and Grant Batty reminisce over their many tours and tests together. *Photograph: New Zealand Herald*

kick the ball, Mourie himself stood in midfield and led the All Black forward pack in the first stamping motions of the haka.

So the moment was right, absolutely right in Mourie's mind, for the preconceived diversionary move. But what actually did happen? Well, folks, the actual execution of such plans are often spoiled by human frailties. So it was with Mourie's scheme. Loveridge tapped the ball and passed to a team mate for the move to start. But the forward (we think he should remain nameless), dropped the ball to the turf. The referee therefore blew his whistle for a knock-on and the game stopped for a scrum, leaving four or five All Black forwards conscientiously — but embarrassed and red-faced — performing the haka in midfield, caught in the gaze of every one of the 50,000 crowd, who were, in that moment, all moved to wonder what the devil they were doing.

The moment passed and the game carried on. Not surprisingly, the use of the Maori war-chant as a decoy rugby tactic has not been seen since!

watching a superb game being played out in good conditions. Even without Mourie's idea it was a fun day. The game was a great one with tremendously fast-moving action. Passions were running high, though only in the best sense. Not so much as a clenched fist was even thought about by any of the players.

Graham Mourie played in all this with the idea for the diversionary tactic not forgotten. At the award of a penalty to his team at a place some fifty metres out from the Barbarians' line, Mourie judged the moment to be exact for his new idea to be put into action. As the halfback David Loveridge positioned himself to tap-

Question: Who was the New Zealander good enough to play representative rugby for two provinces in New Zealand and also to run in the 100 metres at an Olympic Games? He subsequently shifted to Australia and made the Australian Commonwealth Games track and field squad, before returning to New Zealand to win a Gold Medal at the 1974 Commonwealth Games in Christchurch.

Answer: Laurie D'Arcy. He was a South Canterbury and Wellington rugby player. He won New Zealand sprint titles and ran for New Zealand

in the 100 metres at the 1972 Munich Olympic Games. After moving to Australia, he returned in its squad to the Commonwealth Games in Christchurch and was part of the team that won the 4 X 100 metres relay.

Just for the Know-all

If you are one of those clever types who think they know it all, try these for size:
When did Eric Tindall play rugby for the Wallabies?
When did Stu Wilson play for the Lions against the All Blacks?
In which tests did Don Clark play in the All Black scrum?
In what year was Grahame Thorne chosen to play for South Africa?
And when did Bruce Robertson play rugby league for New Zealand?
Stumped? Then read on.

All the above sporting facts did actually occur, but not necessarily to the famous names you might assume. Eric Tindall, for instance, was a halfback from the Drummoyne Club in Sydney who played one international for Australia, at Ballymore in Brisbane, against Tonga in 1973. The famous New Zealand double-international sportsman with the same name was Eric Tindill (a slightly different spelling).

Stu Wilson played for the British Lions on their tour of New Zealand in 1966. To be accurate his Christian name is spelt Stewart and he had been Scottish fullback since 1964. Of the disastrous 1966 Lions team in New Zealand he was one of the outstanding players, appearing, in all four tests.

The All Black flanker Don Clark should not be confused with the All Black fullback Don Clarke. Don Clark (without the 'e') was a Cromwell flanker who forced his way into selection for his country in two test matches in 1964 against Australia. His namesake, Don B. Clarke, is of course one of the most famous names in New

Thorne Named As Member Of S. African Team

By T. P. McLEAN

New Zealand's gift to South African Rugby, G. S. Thorne, has won a rare if not unique distinction — he has been named as a member of a 23-strong South African team.

Thorne made the grade after the South African Rugby Board had staged a series of trials at Bloemfontein.

of that year, has disappeared.

By an oddity, his replacement also bears a British name. He is I. Robertson, a Rhodesian.

The 23-man squad whic includes Thorne has bee charged, according to th Johannesburg Star, wit playing a major role in th restoration of South Africa'

One thing Grahame Thorne could do was capture the headlines! Not only was he a fine All Black who nearly played for the Springboks but, years later, he was back in the news as a sports telecaster with a curly hair-do. The curls nearly caused more discussion than his rugby prowess! *Photograph*: New Zealand Herald

75

A further example of the way that rugby can bring friends together. In wartime you never knew if you would ever see your mates again and this shot, taken during a club game at Athletic Park in 1943, shows Bill Firmin (Poneke-Oriental) being greeted by a pal he obviously hadn't seen in quite a while.

Zealand rugby history. The two played together in the 1964 test at Christchurch.

Grahame Thorne's selection for South Africa occurred in 1973, during the years he was living in the republic. Thorne was picked by the full South African selection committee (with Johann Claassen as convenor) as part of a twenty-three-man squad to tour the country internally.

This unique occurrence did not end with Thorne actually playing for South Africa. At the same time as the internal tour was to take place a series of matches in New Zealand was to be played to raise money for the 1974

Commonwealth Games in Christchurch. Thorne was invited to travel to New Zealand for those games along with two other South Africans, Tommy Bedford and Albie Bates. Thorne chose to come to New Zealand and thus the South African team toured without him. The chance to play for the full Springboks eluded Thorne and he returned to New Zealand permanently in 1974.

The Bruce Robertson who played rugby league is not the same man who played rugby union for New Zealand. The Robertson of rugby league fame was, in his time, the youngest New Zealander to play test league. Young Bruce, an Aucklander, was only eighteen on his test debut on the tour of the United Kingdom in 1951–2. He was the younger brother of the captain of that team, Morrie Robertson.

Two other examples of New Zealand sportsmen with the same name spring to mind. Peter Whiting of Auckland was a New Zealand rugby player in the early seventies while Peter Whiting of Wellington was an international for New Zealand at the sport of soccer in the sixties. He had several years with an English club, Charlton Athletic.

One of the most illustrious names of New Zealand cricket, John Reid, has a modern double. The older Reid, a cricketing giant, played for his country from 1949 until 1965. The younger John made his cricket debut for New Zealand as a youngster and then was dropped for several seasons. By 1984 he was back in the team and celebrated his return with an excellent tour of Sri Lanka, compiling a top score of 180 in the third test at Colombo. That was a total which 'old' John Reid (no relation) never attained in a test.

Kenny's Comeback

Perhaps the most inspirational sporting story to come out of the Second World War concerns H. W. (Mick) Kenny. This young Maori was a highly promising footballer, and in 1939 he was tipped to at least emulate the feats of his brother Alma who had been both a Wellington and New Zealand Maori representative. Sometime after the outbreak of hostilities Mick was sent on the Middle East campaign. There he got in the way of a burst of fire from a German machine-gun and suffered wounds that were so serious that it was feared he might not even survive, let alone play rugby again.

Mick Kenny had been well thought of in Army rugby in Egypt and was on the short list for the 1945–6 Kiwi tour of the United Kingdom. But his wounds meant that all thoughts of rugby were put behind him. He was sent home by hospital ship.

Once back in Wellington Mick Kenny began the long, long, journey back to health and fitness. One paper at the time described the machine-gun holes in his body as being 'big enough to bury your fist in'. But Mick Kenny did come back.

Three years after being wounded, and at nearly thirty years of age, Mick Kenny played for the Wellington representative team in 1948. His form as a fullback was very good, superb if you consider the seriousness of his wounds, and soon the New Zealand Maori selectors expressed an interest in the burly, big-kicking attacking player. So it came about that Mick toured Australia in 1949 with the New Zealand Maori team, thus matching his brother. Mick's comeback was complete and those who had seen him suffer in the intervening years could hardly credit his courage and tenacity.

I have known Mick Kenny for many years now, but he has never spoken to me of his wartime experiences. His modesty almost matches the enormous courage he showed after that burst of gunfire that could so easily have robbed New Zealand of one of its bravest sporting sons.

Question: Can you identify this All Black from the clues given? He was in his time a most controversial selection as All Blacks fullback. He had the Christian names of Graham Duncan McMillan and was Scottish born. He scored a massive 135 points from the fullback berth on his only tour. But he disappeared from view as an All Black soon after returning home. Who was he?

Answer: He was born Graham Duncan McMillan Gilbert, but in all his sport he was known as Mike Gilbert. He made the 1935–6 All Blacks as fullback ahead of hot competition which included the legendary George Nepia. Gilbert was a great success on that tour, playing in all the internationals and being the team's number one goal-kicker. He later turned to rugby league.

Last Laugh for Bebb

The Welsh and British Isles rugby winger Dewi Bebb must have had many a sleepless night as he recalled his play in the third test of 1966 between the Lions and the All Blacks

Dewi Bebb's rugby disaster at Christchurch, 1966. Better things were to come years later.

at Lancaster Park in Christchurch. At one point of that game the Lions team, having lost the first two tests (without having scored so much as one try!), were in with a reasonable chance of beating the All Blacks. The ball spun out along the British backline, the All Black defence was broken and out on the wing was Dewi Bebb.

The New Zealand goal line ahead was open, unguarded and almost begging for a try to be scored when the ball was passed to the Welshman. But in a teeth-grinding moment Bebb spilled the ball forward, the Lancaster Park crowd was scornful in its traditional manner, and Bebb was left with a lost chance and ultimately another lost test match.

Dewi Bebb returned to Lancaster Park in 1971 as a television reporter for Harlech Television. Overseas rights for the Lions tour had been sold to the BBC, so Harlech had to be satisfied with 'news access', which meant that they could screen up to a maximum of two minutes of any match as a news item.

Not daunted by memories of his 1966 blunder, Bebb and his hired New Zealand film crew set up to film the second test match for his meagre quota of highlights. Elsewhere the NZBC set in electronic cameras at what they reckoned were the best vantage points.

As you may recall, New Zealand won the game by 22 points to 12 and the high point was a scorching try scored by the All Black flanker Ian Kirkpatrick who pushed off Lion after Lion in a fifty-metre rush to the line.

In the full telecast the NZBC cameras, in black and white coverage, show Kirkpatrick bursting away from the opposition forwards. But the view is too close up and was shot from too low an angle to see the magnificence of Kirkpatrick as he outflanked the Lions' defensive scheme. Only too late was a wide shot shown to demonstrate how far Kirkpatrick had to go or where the defenders were. It's a risk that every TV director takes during a live telecast. And the truth is that on this occasion NZBC made a mess of it.

Meanwhile, up on their lofty perch overlooking the park, the film crew shooting for Harlech had their camera in a perfect position to see the action. The film they shot showed the 'Kirky' run to the best of its awesome power, and revealed perfectly just how hard he was moving, where he was in relation to the defenders and how far he had to go. And the Harlech film was not shot in the Stygian gloom of black-and-white as was NZBC's. Theirs was crystal-clear colour as well!

Dewi Bebb, therefore, must smile to himself today as he recalls his 'other' memory of Lancaster Park, New Zealand. His satisfaction was complete, no doubt, when his coverage of the golden moment was later sold back (at a healthy rate one hopes) to the New Zealand television authorities.

So when coverage of Kirkpatrick's try is played on New Zealand television (as it is every so often), remember this. If you are seeing it in black-and-white, that is the official version. If it is in colour then that is the Harlech TV version, and somewhere in deepest darkest Wales likeable Dewi Bebb, the man who was scoffed at in 1966, is smiling.

Question: *When did the All Blacks play a match on tour refereed by one of their own team?*

Answer: *At the end of the 1928 All Black tour of South Africa New Zealand played an unofficial match against Combined Capetown Universities. The referee was Jim Burrows, the All Black front-row forward who was not required in the New Zealand XV that day. By all accounts he did a fine job. New Zealand won 14–9!*

The scorer of a magnificent try at Lancaster Park in 1971 — Ian Kirkpatrick.

79

Last Word from America

When in 1980 the All Blacks crushed the USA 53–6 in San Diego, the game was fully reported by the New Zealand pressmen in attendance. The most memorable quote, however, came from the typewriter of Dan Levin, who was more accustomed to reporting on baseball and American football. In *Sports Illustrated* he wrote:

The final score was All Blacks 53, USA Eagles 6, which was one point closer than the last time the two teams had met in 1913. In that year New Zealand won by 51–3. On the scale of improvement shown by the USA in 1980, the United States can expect to draw a game against New Zealand in the year 5129!

Managers

One of the more difficult and sometimes controversial tasks in the sporting world is that of managing an overseas touring rugby team passing through the country. Many have been the managers who have toured New

Zealand and been rated 'disasters' by officials, writers and rugby folk.

Some managers become as infamous as their most notorious players. For instance, few members of the 1930 British rugby team are recalled to mind as quickly as their manager 'Bim' Baxter. It was he who, when told that the rival game rugby league was quite popular in Auckland, replied that 'every city must have its sewer'.

The most sensational rugby team manager incident in New Zealand occurred in 1931. Mr Tom Davis was the appointed leader of the Wallabies and he performed his tour functions adequately — for a time. One day, though, Mr Davis suddenly left for home, having had enough, it seemed, of the players under his command and the regimen of the touring way of life. One of the players, Bryan Palmer (who had broken his leg), took over the managerial role until the end of the tour.

Outsiders watching the tour wondered why Mr Davis left for home so suddenly and mysteriously. So too did members of the Wallaby team. 'He never told us why,' said Bryan Palmer to *The Australian* in 1982. 'None of us knows to this day.'

Was Mr Davis greatly disappointed in the performance of his team? Perhaps. The Australians had won only one match out of six while he was at the helm. But under Bryan Palmer's temporary leadership they won three of their last five games and outscored the All Blacks three tries to two, losing the only test at Auckland because of a superb goal-kicking display by the New Zealand fullback Ron Bush.

Question: *Why was the All Black Jack Manchester nicknamed 'Tarzan' on the 1934 All Black tour of Australia?*

Answer: *Although it may seem odd in these days of weird haircuts, Jack Manchester's hairstyle in 1934 was considered rebellious. It was parted cleanly down the centre and slicked back, just like Tarzan of the Apes in the movies. Jack Manchester later assumed the nickname 'Lugger' because of the disastrous effect which scrummaging had had on his ears!*

Manawatu's Walloping

When Manawatu won the 1980 New Zealand rugby provincial championship it was a popular victory for the green and whites. They had a strong team, blessed with fast sturdy backs and tough forwards. In the team photograph taken at the season's end there are no fewer than nine All Blacks looking proudly out, plus another six

My word, they had style those 1905 All Blacks! Here, fullback George Gillett, kicking for goal, is complete with a large Army belt and a hat to shield his eyes from the English sun. His ball-holder, captain Dave Gallaher, is also trend-setting with shin pads outside his socks.

or seven who had or have since represented New Zealand in Colts, Juniors, Maori or University teams.

Over the 1980 season the Manawatu team improved steadily. Their coach, Graham Hamer, had originally hoped for a fourth placing in the Division One championship series, but after a slow start the team won the title with only one loss out of fourteen games against the best of New Zealand provincial rugby.

When the 1981 season rolled around, Manawatu, as New Zealand's champion team, were the target of several invitations to play special matches before settling down to defend their title in the new season. The most attractive offer came from across the Tasman. New South Wales is traditionally a strong state side but Manawatu agreed to play them. They must have felt confident enough about their chances of winning the special match.

Graham Hamer chose a twenty-one-man touring squad based on his winning team of the previous season and when the teams took the field for the game at Sydney's T. G. Milner Field, the Manawatu team contained no fewer than six All Blacks. Mark Donaldson, Gary Knight, Geoff Old, Doug Rollerson, Ken Granger and Mark Shaw were there. The New South Wales side contained the three Ella brothers — Mark, Glen and Gary — plus seven other Wallaby players. In other words, there were enough good players on either side to make it a good hard tight game of the very best international quality.

The final score of 58–3 to New South Wales was, when first heard, not believed by many New Zealanders. Rugby pride could not conceive that such a score was possible. The other way round perhaps. But never 58–3 against the New Zealand provincial champions!

Yet it was true. And there were no excuses offered by Manawatu. Their captain, Mark Donaldson, told reporters afterwards that he had never experienced anything like it in rugby before. 'I'm at a loss to explain what happened.'

What happened was simply one of the most one-sided hidings ever dished out to a top New Zealand provincial side. The Ella brothers were superb, ducking and diving through the Manawatu players who, to their credit, tried hard throughout and never gave up.

New South Wales scored ten tries, four of them by the speedy winger Mick Martin. Between them the Ella brothers scored 15 points and on the wing Laurie Monoghan converted six of the tries. Manawatu limped home, with five players showing minor injuries, such was the force of the blitz they had faced.

And, true to form, they had had to face some wicked taunts from the crowd of 5000 who had turned out to see the match. 'Why didn't you send over Manawa-one?' yelled one hard-cased fan while near the end of the game, when the score had passed 50, the New Zealand players had to endure, 'Hey, you Kiwis, why didn't you let your husbands play?'

Mother's Boys

This story, first recounted by Peter Devlin in the *Auckland Star* in August of 1972, tells of the disastrous influence which the mother of the great All Blacks Colin and Stan Meads could have had on their rugby careers had she fulfilled a threat she made to the two brothers.

It all happened long before both Colin or Stan became All Blacks. It involved their being picked to oppose each other in two trial matches to pick the King Country representative team.

'There was trouble in the first line-out of the first trial,' said Colin. 'For some reason or other Stanley swung a punch which landed fair and square on me and laid me on my back. Next line-out I grabbed Stan as he went up for the ball and heaved. He went down on his back. From there on it was a real

donnybrook between the two of us. We fought our way through the trial.'

'Afterwards, for days, it was the same at home. Not fighting but a bitter silence as we went about our farm work. Finally on the day, a week later, when we were to play the second trial, our Mum stepped in. At breakfast she laid down an ultimatum to Stan and me; if we didn't shake hands and forget our nonsense she promised to walk on to the field after the match started, take an ear in each hand and lead us off.'

'Stan and I both knew that was the end of the argument. We shook hands because we knew darn well she would have done it!'

In later years there wasn't a man in the rugby world who would have even countenanced the thought of taking such actions with the much-feared Meads brothers. Still, it makes for an interesting thought . . .

Question: In which international rugby tour match in New Zealand did an ambulance drive on to the playing field to remove a seriously injured player?

Answer: British Isles v. Taranaki 1977. The injured man was none other than David Loveridge, later to become an All Black captain and long-standing test halfback.

The ambulance spent nearly 15 minutes on the field at Rugby Park in New Plymouth, removing Loveridge with what looked like a serious knee injury. Love-ridge had other ideas, however. He was back, albeit on crutches, later that evening in time for the after-match party, and he played again not too many weeks later.

Oddities

The list of All Blacks who never toured is hardly ever added to in these days of frequent travelling overseas. But in the 1960s two All Blacks were regular and vital members of the national team yet never made a tour away for their country. Ron Rangi played ten test matches as a centre in the years 1964–6. His appearances were all consecutive but after being banned from the All Blacks for a year in 1967 (a bizarre story in itself) Rangi never again made the All Blacks.

Mick Williment, the Wellington fullback, was a close challenger to Rangi's record. Williment was an outstanding All Black in the same years as Rangi. By playing high-class test rugby Williment softened the blow caused by the retirement of the great D. B. Clarke. But, like Rangi, Williment's internationals were all played inside New Zealand. After nine tests, eight of which were victories, Williment was a surprise omission from the 1967 All Blacks tour of Canada, the United Kingdom and France. The rise of his replacement, Fergie McCormick, meant Williment too was not required for his country again and thus he and Rangi retired, to head the list of 'home' All Blacks.

The man who had most tours in the national rugby colours while not achieving test-match status was the Northland looseman Bevan Holmes. He made four official tours with the All Blacks, two around New Zealand in 1972 and 1973 and one each to South Africa (1970) and the United Kingdom (1972–3). In all, Holmes played thirty-one matches for his country, and while he was never asked

The New Zealand sporting public loved Colin Meads so much that when Meads (*extreme left*) lowered the Welsh hooker Jeff Young in this Christchurch test in 1969, many were the Kiwis who said, 'Young ought never to have deliberately crashed his jaw into Meads' fist'! *Photograph by Peter Bush*

to play a test match, he did achieve one unusual honour — *en route* to South Africa in 1970 he played twice for the All Blacks on one day! It was in Perth when the thirty-man New Zealand squad stopped to play Western Australia.

Holmes played the curtain-raiser for New Zealand against the local President's XV and later came on as a replacement for New Zealand in the main game against Western Australia. On the same day his team mate Bruce Hunter, the Otago winger, played both games in full, the only All Black to achieve that rare feat.

Question: When did the All Blacks play a rugby test match over four quarters instead of the customary two halves?

Answer: At Athletic Park in 1913, New Zealand's All Blacks played the Australian test team over four twenty-minute spells. This was because of the extremely cold, wet and muddy condition of the ground. Hot drinks warmed the players at each break and some players changed to dry clothing. New Zealand won the game by 30 points to 5 after leading by 11 to 5 at half-time. The players did not change ends at the quarter-time breaks.

The glory of the winter game in New Zealand: a sheet of water hides the scorer of this try at Athletic Park in Wellington. Perhaps whoever he is should be called 'the unknown warrior of New Zealand rugby', in tribute to all those muddied, waterlogged men of years gone by — and years to come. *Photograph: Evening Post*

Off!

If a sports freak ever approaches you and asks you to name the New Zealander who was the first rugby player to be sent home, for disciplinary reasons, from an international tour of the United Kingdom, do not rush into saying that the man was Keith Murdoch. While it is true that Murdoch was dismissed from the 1972–3 All Black tour after an incident in a Cardiff Hotel following the Welsh international, he was not the first New Zealander to have been treated thus.

Not many years earlier, a young New Zealander from Taumaranui had gone to Australia to find work and play rugby. His name was Ross Cullen and his footballing talent was such that

soon he was in the East Brisbane senior club side and was made captain. Better things followed for young Cullen. In 1966 his excellent play moved the Wallaby selectors to give him a tour place as a hooker in the Australian team which was then to undertake a thirty-six-match tour of the northern hemisphere.

On tour in the United Kingdom it was expected that Cullen would play as second-string hooker to the great Peter Johnson. However, the selectors gave Cullen the first tour match against North East Counties at Gosforth. There, the team crashed to a 14–17 defeat, although Cullen had a reasonable debut in the front row. Peter Johnson played the second tour match, a 17–9 win over Midland

Counties at Leicester, but it was Cullen who was selected to play in the third game against Oxford University.

That game kicked off in overcast conditions on the pretty Iffley Road ground at Oxford and the action settled down to a close battle. It seems from newspaper reports that as the game progressed some of the Wallaby forwards became irritated with the University prop forward Oliver ('Ollie') Waldron, an ex-Irish international. The Australians felt that some of Waldron's forward play was over-vigorous and there were a few words spoken though no major outbreaks of fighting occurred.

The match was nearing its end when suddenly, after a scrum, Waldron staggered away clutching his ear. Blood was pouring from a wound and attendants noted that his ear-lobe was badly torn. He was encouraged by the first-aid people to leave the field. No action was taken on the field about whatever had happened to Waldron. The game went on to its conclusion and Australia won by 11 points to 9.

Underneath the grandstand afterwards the Australian manager, Mr Bill McLaughlin, went into the Oxford dressing-room and asked about Waldron's condition. There he was told that the big Irishman's injury had been caused by a bite and that the culprit was one of the Australian team.

It was not until later in the evening that Ross Cullen was asked by Mr McLaughlin if he had been the offender. Cullen admitted biting Waldron in a scrum and the next morning he was dismissed from the tour. He journeyed back to London on his own and flew back to Australia. He never played first-class rugby again.

Naturally there was a storm in the press over the incident, and many times the fact that Cullen was a New Zealander was noted. The punishment had been the most severe rugby penalty since 1925 when Cyril Brownlie, also of New Zealand, was sent off in the All Blacks match against England at Twickenham.

According to the newspapers I have read recently, Ross Cullen acted with great openness over the incident. He freely admitted the biting action but claimed it to be just part of the battle that had been waged that day between the tough Waldron and the touring team. What was the most debatable point for rugby people was whether the Australian manager should have taken the action he did. After all, it was argued, the referee (who according to all rugby law is the 'sole judge of fact' on the field) did not even issue a warning.

McLaughlin had had only a view from the grandstand many metres away. Ross Cullen returned to Brisbane where his club immediately labelled him a 'gentleman' and stood firmly by their man. Years later it was reported that Cullen had returned to live in his native New Zealand, although this has never been confirmed.

The only obvious difference between the Ross Cullen incident and the later Keith Murdoch affair was that Murdoch was a very familiar figure to New Zealanders, whereas Cullen was not, so that when Murdoch came back to New Zealand he was hounded incessantly by media people for his version of events and left the country. Cullen, it seems, was allowed his privacy.

Incidentally, in the 1983 *Rothmans Australian Rugby Yearbook* there is a historical section, one part of which details those New Zealanders by birth who have played for Australia. In a list of over twenty names there is no mention of Ross Cullen, formerly of Taumaranui. His omission takes on a slightly sinister look when it is also noted that another expatriate Kiwi is not included: the Wellingtonian Rod Kelleher who toured South Africa with the Wallabies in 1969. When it is recalled that Kelleher was sent off for fighting in the Australia versus Rhodesia match, one wonders whether the Australian Rugby Union or some of its historians have deliberately expunged those two players' names from their records.

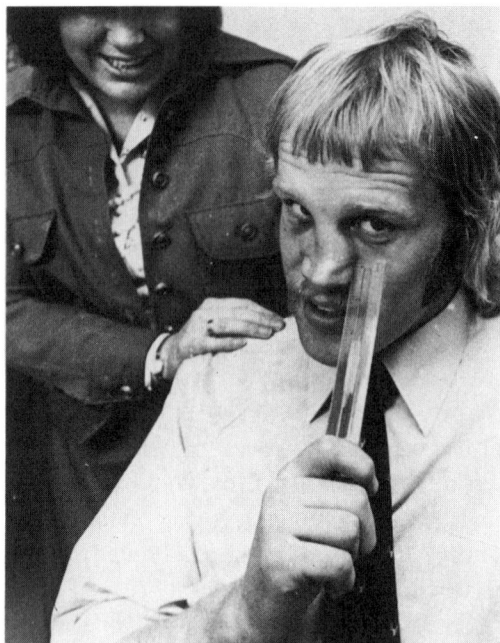

Ian Turley was not responsible for this one, but my word, somebody or something has hit All Black Gary Seear a beauty — right on the button! *Photograph* : Otago Daily Times

Pick of the Punches

Obviously, this one is debatable, but was the best punch ever landed on a New Zealand rugby field the one thrown by Ian Turley of Wairarapa-Bush at the British Isles' Nigel Horton in 1977?

Maybe. Maybe not. All that must be said is that Turley's big swing on Horton was a hummer, a blockbuster, a peach of a punch, call it what you will.

It came when the Lions of 1977 played their opening tour game at Memorial Park, Masterton. Horton was the big Englishman who had come to New Zealand with the reputation of a tough character. According to the local players Horton was throwing his weight about until Turley, a big farmer, swung his hammer Horton's way.

The punch, begun as a big swing, connected with Horton flush on the face and down went the big Englishman. In the moments that fol-

lowed he lay face down on the ground, oblivious to where he was, his reputation as a tough guy in tatters. He rose to his hands and knees but then collapsed again into the mud. Horton was led off the field, was put up in a Masterton hospital overnight, and missed the next two tour games.

While one must, naturally, frown on such behaviour during the course of a rugby match, Ian Turley's punch that day was one to remember. I'll wager Nigel Horton has never forgotten it.

Ranfurly on the Move

'The Ranfurly Shield — the very mention of the words causes the blood of the average New Zealander to flow a little quicker and the pulse to beat faster.' With those words the well-known rugby statistician of yesteryear, Arthur Carman, opened his book recording the history of Ranfurly Shield rugby in New Zealand.

Even in modern times, with the distractions of other sports and other rugby competitions, the Ranfurly Shield still retains a grip on imagination of New Zealanders. Each season when a team challenges the shield-holder, grown men and women, young children as well, become crazed with provincial fervour for their team. It has become a New Zealand tradition to journey from one's own province to be at the ground to witness the challenge, no matter how arduous the journey.

Perhaps the craziest season of Ranfurly Shield history came in 1950 when there were five matches and five holders of the shield. Such movement of this much-valued sporting trophy over any one season has not been repeated before or since.

In 1949 Otago had brilliantly defended the shield. That was the year when Fred Allen led an All Black tour of South Africa and eleven Otago men were in the touring party. Yet the stay-at-homes from Dunedin and its surrounds had held off challenges from six strong unions, and with their top men home again Otago was expected to easily repel all challenges in 1950. But it was not to be, and 1950 became the strangest year yet for Ranfurly Shield upsets.

Otago started off with their nineteenth defence in a row against their arch-rivals Southland. In a fast-moving match in front of a 30,000 crowd, Otago's nine All Blacks, past or current, hammered the men from the south and sent them home with a 22–3

hiding. Otago really clicked that day, spearheaded by Laurie Haig in the backs and Kevin Skinner in the forwards. And afterwards, challengers from the North Island were regarded as having no hope at all of lifting the Shield.

Nine days later Canterbury challenged. Otago made three changes but still announced a side that looked far too good on paper for the red and blacks. On the day, a very wet and rainy one, Otago took first use of the wind and driving rain, but surprised and disappointed the 12,000 fans who had braved the weather by not scoring at all. In the second half the crowd was stunned into silence as the magnificent Canterbury forwards swept the field in rush after rush. Peter Kearney, the challengers' first-five, dashed over for a try at the end of one such rush and eight minutes later Kearney made a try for the centre Tommy Lynch. The game ended and Canterbury had shocked the entire country by beating Otago 8–0 and breaking the grip that Otago and Southland had had on the Shield for fifteen years.

Canterbury took the shield home to Christchurch and looked upon its first

challenge, from Wairarapa, with ease of mind. Wairarapa was weak, very weak. But when they played Canterbury with the shield at stake the men in green played like men possessed. There was only one score in the whole eighty minutes. Shortly before half time the Wairarapa fullback Mahapuku landed a glorious field-goal from halfway. Not too many people at Lancaster Park were overworried when the challengers led 3–0 at half-time. But forty minutes later, when Mr Broadhead, the referee from Wanganui, blew his whistle for full time, the shield was on the move again! Wairarapa, by virtue of its bustling play, had won by that solitary dropped goal to nil.

Naturally, back home in Masterton the people were rapt. It had been twenty-one long years since the shield had resided in those parts. They even displayed Mahapuku's boot like it was some treasure found from ancient days. But Wairarapa was to have the shield for only fourteen days before it was to lose it to the first challenge.

On 16 September, South Canterbury turned it on in front of 6000 people at the Solway Showgrounds. They won an excellent match 17–14, thanks above all to Timaru's two brilliant All Blacks Lachie Grant and Morrie Goddard.

Masterton was sad, Timaru proud. It was the first (ever) win for South Canterbury in a shield match. But the Ranfurly Shield was destined to be constantly on the move in 1950 and South Canterbury could not stop the fates. They too had possession of the trophy for exactly a fortnight. When Ted Griffin's North Aucklanders came to town, the Log of Wood moved again.

North Auckland had gambled on winning and had spent £1000 in getting their team to Timaru for the match which was a special challenge.

When the teams took the field there was a record crowd of 18,000 at Fraser Park. Yet again it was the challengers who won through, and North Auckland took the shield home, after winning 20–9. As this match had been played on the last possible day for shield challenges, the Log of Wood stayed for the summer in Whangarei.

So several Ranfurly Shield records were established in 1950. Five different unions held the shield. For the first time it journeyed back and forth between the North and South Islands *twice* in the one season. For the first time in a season three holders had lost the shield to the first challenger, two unions had won the shield for the first time, and for the first time two holders failed to score when trying to ward off a challenge.

SPORTSQUOTE

Problems with Wales

'Grounded ball six inches over line. Some of the Welsh players admit try. Hunter and Glasgow can confirm was pulled back before referee arrived. Deans.' This was the telegram sent by All Black Bob Deans in 1905 to the London *Daily Mail* confirming that he felt he had scored against Wales. As Deans was a man of impeccable trust and honour, these words have been the basis of New Zealand claims that he was illegally deprived of a try.

POST OFFICE TELEGRAPHS.

If the Receiver of an Inland Telegram doubts its accuracy, he may have it repeated on payment of half the amount originally paid for its transmission, any fraction of 1d. less than ½d. being reckoned as ½d.; and if it be found that there was any inaccuracy, the amount paid for repetition will be refunded. Special conditions are applicable to the repetition of Foreign Telegrams.

Office Stamp.

Charges to pay £ s. d.

Handed in at *Cardiff* at *10 26* M. Received here at

TO{ *Daily Mail Lndn*

grounded Ball 6 inches over
line some of welsh players
admit try Hunter and Glasgow
can confirm was pulled back
by welsh men before Referee arrived
Deans

This reminds me of that evergreen quote attributed to Graham Mourie: 'You never beat the Welsh at rugby, you just score more points.' Why do I say evergreen? Because the same words have been attributed to two other All Blacks — captain Ian Kirkpatrick and halfback Kevin Briscoe.

Question: A rugby match with a final score of 14–12 looks like a game of very few tries. Yet when the North Island beat the South Island by that margin at Athletic Park in Wellington in 1951, how many tries were there in the match?

Answer: No less than 8. The North Island scored 4, with one conversion for their 14 points. The South scored 4 unconverted tries. (A try was worth only 3 points in those days.)

Schoolboys Dish Out a Lesson

Many have been the times when the mighty All Blacks, giants of men, have used their brute and brawn to humble the best of rugby teams assembled to play them. Everywhere rugby is played in the world, a mere mention of the name 'All Blacks' brings instant respect from local people as they recall occasions when New Zealand's rugby players have dished out a lesson to their own team.

But even the most blinkered Kiwi rugby fan has to admit that once in a while things have not gone entirely his team's way. And one of the more intriguing defeats for the New Zealand rugby team came in 1935 at St Helens Ground in Swansea, Wales.

The home team, nicknamed the All Whites, were pretty inexperienced that year, especially in the positions of

scrum half and fly half, so their selectors looked beyond the available adult talent in that 'lovely, ugly' town, as Dylan Thomas so fondly called Swansea.

Eventually two cousins from Gowerton County School, Haydn Tanner and Willie Davies, were invited by Swansea to play in their team to meet the All Blacks captained by Jack Manchester. Both were teenagers, one aged seventeen the other eighteen, and on 28 September they ran on to St Helens to face the mighty men of New Zealand. (Photographs of the 1935 All Blacks show them to have been a fearsome-looking squad. None more so than their captain, Jack Manchester, whose cauliflowered ears, beetled brow and rugged visage were an example for all 'toughies' of the day to aspire to match!)

If the two youngsters, Tanner and Davies, were in awe of the All Blacks they never showed it, as both played with an absolute freedom of youthful

spirit and dazzled their illustrious opponents. Their combination was the most vital factor in Swansea's 11–3 win — the only victory the club has ever had over the All Blacks.

As the All Blacks trooped off the field the realisation of what had happened to them was epitomised in a remark Jack Manchester made to a local pressman. 'You can tell the people back home what you like, but just don't tell them the All Blacks were beaten today by a couple of schoolboys!'

Test Fever

The strength and hold that the sport of rugby has on the population of New Zealand is sometimes astonishing. Consider this story from a rugby test day a few years back.

At a police station in one of our major cities all was quiet. So quiet in fact that the policemen on duty hoped they would be able to view undisturbed the rugby match on television that afternoon. But early in the afternoon a call came into the station saying that a man's body had been found inside a city building. The police went to investigate.

On the scene it was soon ascertained that the body was that of an elderly vagrant who had quite obviously died peacefully in his sleep. But certain procedures had to be put into action by the police squad, as is the usual case in a sudden death. The real problem was that kick-off time in the test match loomed.

Thinking quickly, the squad sealed off the building where the body lay. They closed off the street outside. They annouced to the media that a murder investigation inquiry had begun. And they posted a soccer-playing officer to keep watch. Then the rugby fans of the squad returned to the station to watch the excitement of the test match, arriving just in time for the kick-off.

Afterwards they returned to the site of the 'murder', sifted through some relevant material, and declared to the world that they were now satisfied that the old man had died naturally!

Top Score

Most points by a senior rugby union player in any one match in New Zealand were scored by a Central Otago man, Ralph Milne, in 1982. Taking the field at a tiny place called Poolburn, Milne played on the wing for his club Matakanui Valley when their senior team played Alexandra B. 'Pity the poor "Bs"', you might say. They got crunched by 108 points to 3 with winger Milne scoring 9 tries and kicking 12 conversions for a total of 60 points.

This picture *(top right)* shows a classic example of the New Zealand All Blacks' not-quite-universal popularity wherever they play. This try, scored by Stu Wilson in Swansea in1978, was from a glorious back movement that swept 50 metres. Yet there's not one look of admiration from the Welshmen watching! *Photograph by Peter Bush*

Below right Mind you, the New Zealanders at Lancaster Park in Christchurch during this test match against Australia in1978 look pretty deadpan about things as well; they're probably wondering what the Aussies are coming up with next. The 'up the jumper' move was a rugby rarity but when it worked well no one knew where the ball was. *Photograph:* The Press, *Christchurch*

Only an Englishman who scored 64 points is recorded as ever having done better in a senior-status match.

TV Breakthrough

The first-ever live telecast of a rugby game in New Zealand was on 27 June 1967 at Athletic Park in Wellington.

The two teams were Wellington College and St Patrick's College (Town). St Pat's won 9–8. The New Zealand Rugby Union had resisted live television for years, but ironically it was the son of the chairman of the New Zealand Union, John L. Sullivan (see insert photograph), who scored the try that opened the score for St Pat's that day.

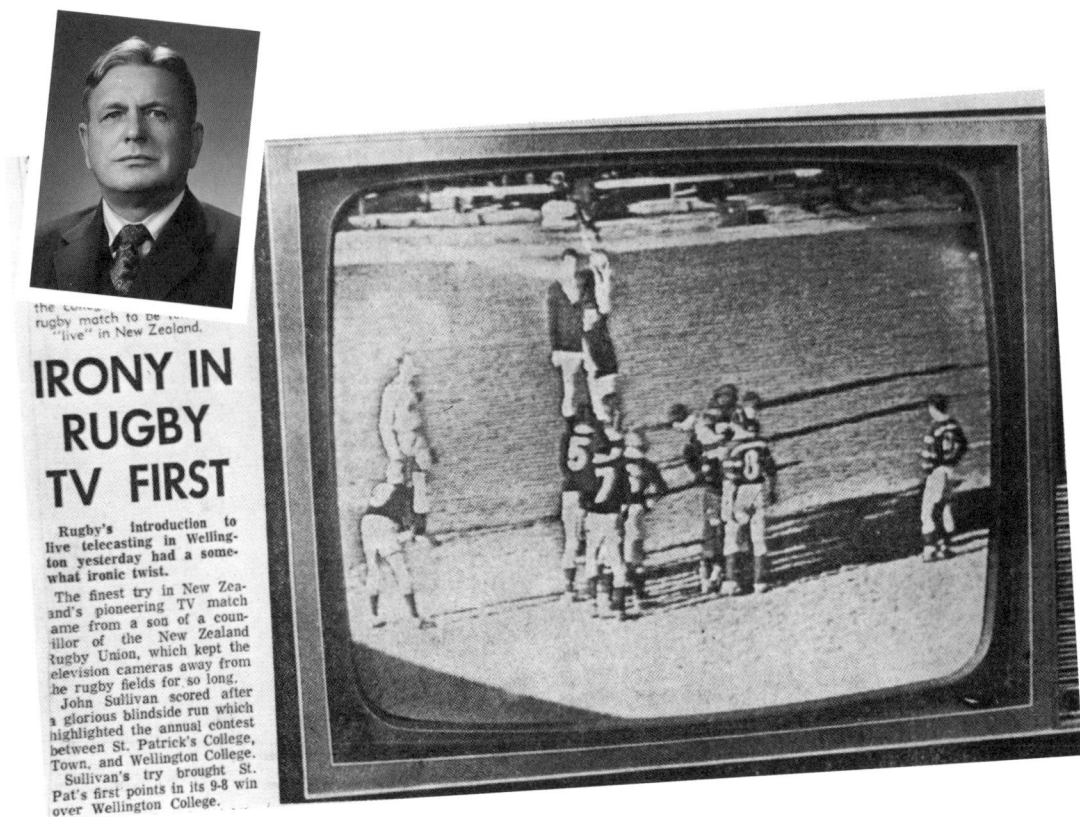

IRONY IN RUGBY TV FIRST

Rugby's introduction to live telecasting in Wellington yesterday had a somewhat ironic twist.

The finest try in New Zealand's pioneering TV match came from a son of a councillor of the New Zealand Rugby Union, which kept the television cameras away from the rugby fields for so long.

John Sullivan scored after a glorious blindside run which highlighted the annual contest between St. Patrick's College, Town, and Wellington College. Sullivan's try brought St. Pat's first points in its 9-8 win over Wellington College.

Wilson and Wilson

There was nothing untoward happening in a game between Athletic and Poneke until a flare-up of fists broke out among the forwards of the two teams. When one of the Poneke men was laid out and did not get up the referee turned to the Athletic players and asked, rather sternly, which one of them was to blame.

In those days one presumes that to such a question an answer was definitely required, and honour and honesty being what it was a man's word was never to be doubted.

According to the story Arthur 'Ranji' Wilson, the famous All Black of 1908–14, was the culpable party in the Athletic forward pack that day. He, however, was an important member of the club's team and of the Wellington reps and was also a dead-cert selection for the All Black team. He was needed.

What happened, then, to this request by the referee for the striker of the Poneke man to identify himself? It seems that William Wilson, a brother of Ranji and known as Wally to his colleagues and mates, was the first to sum up the seriousness of the situation should 'Ranji' be sent from the field. Penalties for such fighting were tough in those days and the Poneke man still lay stiff and stark. And the referee waited.

Wally Wilson eventually stepped forward and gallantly offered that it was he who had offended. He was promptly sent from the field and in the days that followed his 'case' was discussed by the Wellington rugby union. Finally he was, quite sadly one feels, suspended from the game for life.

Ranji Wilson played on in the sport of rugby union and the next season continued his career as New Zealand's top loose forward. In all he represented New Zealand over four seasons. His brother Wally, banished from the fifteen-aside game, resumed his sporting activity in rugby league and was soon good enough to play for New Zealand. So too did another brother, Sim.

It is not recorded what either brother involved in the incident thought about it in later years. Nor are the injured Poneke man's opinions recorded, it should be added. Ranji died in 1953 after a long and proud association with the rugby game, having been an All Black of great standing as well as a New Zealand selector.

Incidentally, his nickname came from his coloured skin. To New Zealanders he was easily identifiable as not being of Maori stock, so Ranji sufficed as his name, probably in the belief that he was of Indian parentage. In fact the brothers were neither, having been born of English-West Indian stock.

Wally Wilson lived a hale and hearty life too, outliving his older brother by nearly twenty years and dying in the early 1970s.

SOCCER

'Anzac Ashes'

One wonders whether the victorious New Zealand soccer team of 1981, having beaten Australia on the Sydney Cricket Ground 2–0 on its way to the World Cup finals in Spain, knew that somewhere in Australia is a trophy once presented for competition between the two countries. The trophy, a splendid combination of mounted silver on Australian and New Zealand native woods, was first played for in 1933 when the New Zealand team was on tour.

The 'Anzac Ashes' as the prize was called, had interesting beginnings. When the New Zealand team toured Australia in 1923 the two captains dined together at a banquet after each of the three test matches. As the two team leaders, George Campbell of New Zealand and Alex Gibb of Australia, relaxed at the end of their dinner they smoked cigars. The ashes from those cigars were carefully collected by Mr Harry Meyer, the New Zealand team manager. He retained the ashes till he found a suitable container for them. Mr W. Fisher, the Queensland FA Secretary, provided a cigarette case that he had carried through the Gallipoli campaign eight years before. Mr Meyer had the case restored and mounted on New Zealand honeysuckle wood and Australian maple to make a splendid trophy which was then put up for the winner of future matches between the two soccer nations.

There was serious battle for the 'Anzac Ashes' in 1933 (when Australia won three test matches to New Zealand's nil) and in 1936 (again three wins to Australia, none to New Zealand), but by 1948 when Australia toured New Zealand the trophy was not sighted or talked about (just as well perhaps, Australia won 6–0, 7–0, 4–0 and 8–1).

Since then no mention has ever been made of the trophy, at least in New Zealand. Perhaps it was forgotten in New Zealand because of the repeated defeats New Zealand suffered.

It is surprising nevertheless that a call was not made from New Zealand to Australia to find the trophy after New Zealand won against the 'Socceroos' at Auckland in 1979, then again, over the two World Cup matches

in 1981 and two matches in 1983. The 'Anzac Ashes' remain lost to this day, unheard of in New Zealand since 1936.

Soccer Sensations

When youngsters cheered the New Zealand soccer team for reaching the finals of the 1982 World Cup in Spain, there must have been many an old-timer amongst the soccer fans who remembered the dark and difficult days of the past when it was a great achievement just to avoid being thrashed.

Still, New Zealand didn't get off to such a bad start, comparatively speaking. In 1904 New Zealand played two tests against the touring New South Wales team and actually managed to win one of them. Twenty years later they won their first series — though the opposition was not exactly world-champion material, being made up of Chinese university players.

But in 1936 there began the sequence of embarrassingly big scores which fans probably prefer to forget. Consider the following scores:

1936 v. Australia	*lost 1–7*
	lost 0–10
1937 v. English Amateurs	*lost 0–12*
	lost 0–6
	lost 1–12
1947 v. South Africa	*lost 5–6*
	lost 0–6
	lost 3–8
	lost 1–4

(Nearly as many points were scored in that series as were in the four rugby tests between the same two countries in 1949! That series also had disas-

1947 NEW ZEALAND REPRESENTATIVES VERSUS SOUTH AFRICA.
Back: A. J. Harris, V. Smith, O. Cleal, P. O'Malley, L. Beavis. **Centre:** K. Mason, W. Woods, A. Wilkinson, R. Davey, G. Drylie, J. Sharpe, A. Wallace. **Front:** L. Wood, R. Speed, J. R. Sheffield. M. Gordon. G. Smith.

Most New Zealand sporting teams of the old days did their best to look like the All Blacks. These are the 1947 New Zealand soccer players. Like the rugby team of 1949, they lost four straight games to South Africa.

trous consequences for New Zealand.)

1948 v. Australia	lost 0–6
	lost 0–7
	lost 0–4
	lost 1–8
1957 v. F. K. Austria	lost 1–7
	lost 1–7
1961 v. English FA	lost 0–8
	lost 1–6
1968 v. Manchester United	lost 0–11

Perhaps the worst return of all, in terms of money spent and effort outlayed, came from the ambitiously planned world tour by New Zealand in 1964.

The team, captained by Ken Armstrong, set off with round-the-world air tickets and had stopovers scheduled at some of the major soccer venues. The high hopes of at least one success were soon shattered as the sequence of losses, with nary a win in sight, caused the code great embarrassment at home.

The defeats that the 1964 New Zealand soccer team suffered were not always big ones (though one supposes 0–8 against Nottingham Forest was pretty bad) but the shock was that nowhere could the team win a match at all: through Hong Kong, Thailand, Iran, West Germany, Switzerland, England and the east coast of the United States.

Finally, they reached California with just one more game to play and four-teen tour losses to dream on. The San Francisco All Stars were the opposition in the last match. Little was reported back to New Zealand, either at the time or later, about the quality of the local team. Were they weak or strong? Young men or old?

In the end, no one really investi-gated the San Francisco team's qualifi-cations too closely. Everyone involved was too busy celebrating the fact that the New Zealanders actually managed to win a game. In fact the 5–2 winning scoreline was not so much the end of a disastrous tour as an occasion for rap-turous delight amongst the New Zealand players. The win meant that

they could return home to New Zealand with one win at least from their 25,000-mile journey!

Donovan's Day

Whichever the country, it is likely that the most tightly played soccer match of any season is the local cup final. Something about the knockout contest where teams of Davids can beat Goliaths captures soccer fans' interest like no other style of competition.

If New Zealanders over the years have lent an ear to the radio com-mentaries of the English F.A. Cup Final — and in latter years watched it live on TV — they have also had the excitement of their own Cup Final to follow.

Each season, from its beginning in 1923, the Chatham Cup Final was a 'must' on every New Zealand soccer

Question: *When the first soccer club was formed in New Zealand, at Auckland in 1870, why was there a delay of several weeks before they could play their first offi-cial match?*

Answer: *They did not have a ball to play with! One had to be imported from Melbourne.*

team's list of ambitions and dreams for that year.

The first winners, from a knockout competition held in both North and South Islands, was the Seacliff club of Otago. They beat the YMCA of Wellington 3 goals to nil.

Later winners with names that are now long gone from the ersatz-sponsored club names of today included the Harbour Board team of Wellington (winners in 1924), Tramways of Auckland (1929) — Tramurewa of Auckland (1931) and Wellington Hospital (1935). Presumably, the Tramurewa lads were some kind of amalgamation of tram drivers and those who had previously played in Manurewa!

If the New Zealand Cup Final is, like its counterpart in so many places in the world, essentially a test of team unity and togetherness under pressure, it is surely the 1958 New Zealand Chatham Cup Final that the world must look to for one of the finest individual performances.

This was played, as every game was in the old days, at Wellington's Basin Reserve and featured one team from the North Island and one from the South.

Seatoun of Wellington played Christchurch City in the 1958 final and the score was a comfortable win by 7–1 to Seatoun.

The individual performance of which I write came from a twenty-four-year-old English immigrant, John Donovan, playing at centre-forward for Seatoun. He had been in New Zealand for only fifteen months but that day hit the headlines by scoring no fewer than 6 of his team's 7 goals. Certainly it was a record for one man in the Chatham Cup Final (one which has never been threatened since) but this writer thinks 6 goals in a national cup final could well be a record worldwide.

John Donovan's near-perfect game naturally led to that year's Chatham Cup Final being known as 'Donovan's Cup'. Interestingly, scoring so many goals in that cup final did not lead to higher honours in the game for Donovan. Rather, he continued to play only at club level for a number of years. Despite what could have been a world record for one man in a cup final John Donovan's feat went unnoticed by people like the New Zealand selectors. Rather unfairly, his effort has been far too quickly forgotten.

SOFTBALL

Little is Best

When the New Zealand softball team set out for the world championships of 1968, they went with high hopes of doing better than their
impressive third placing in their first appearance at the world series
two years before.

Their team was spearheaded by the Wellington whirlwind Kevin Herlihy who had matured into a fast, deceptive pitcher of immense speed and stamina. With Herlihy 'on the mound' even a win in the world series was a possibility.

In the first-round matches Herlihy was in superb form, but since the team felt it necessary to 'nurse' him along he was rested from pitching in the first-round match against Japan. The Japanese were no threat. Though they were good ball players, their size — or lack of it — proved a drawback and they started very much underdogs against New Zealand *sans* Herlihy.

But the Japanese are nothing if not tenacious and the match drifted along quietly without any score. Concern among the New Zealand team did not rise alarmingly until the bottom of the seventh and final innings was reached and the match was still all-square at nil all! At this point the New Zealand team conceded a hit, then with two errors found themselves fielding to a Japanese team that had the bases loaded.

There was a midfield conference and the New Zealanders decided that Kevin Herlihy, supposedly resting from the game, would have to be brought in to save it. Herlihy appeared and took his place on the mound. The Japanese, however, were awake to the tactical change. For the new Kiwi pitcher they brought in a pinch hitter. This new hitter, one observer has told me, was no more than 1.5 metres tall. Accordingly, his 'strike zone' was much lower to the ground. Normally such a man would not provide too many problems, but for a new pitcher, unwarmed-up, coming in to a pressured situation, this represented a whole host of new problems and called for adjustments to established speed and technique.

Herlihy threw his first pitch to the new man. 'Ball!' was called. The same call came to the next two pitches leaving one more chance for New Zealand to save the situation, and the match. Herlihy wound up, the pitch rocketed over the homeplate. But again the call of 'Ball!' was heard. The pitch to the tiny man had been too high. Thus he was awarded a walk to first base. The rest of the Japanese runners on base moved around one. The man on third base was therefore 'walked home'. And as the New Zealand players hung their heads the Japanese danced with joy at their 1–0 upset.

That result effectively put New Zealand out of the 1968 world series finals.

TENNIS

The 1967 women's singles final at the New Zealand championships went down in tennis history as something remarkable, if only because the combined ages of the two 'ladies' in the final added up to a mere thirty-one years!

From a solid field of players fifteen-year-old Marilyn Pryde made it through to the grand final to play sixteen-year-old Anne Stevens. Although records of this type are probably not ever kept, no one at the time, or since, has ever heard of a national tennis final anywhere in the world having a lesser combined total of ages.

Naturally, for a pair so young, there were some nervous moments when the final started in December 1967 at Wilding Park in Christchurch. Anne Stevens suffered the worst of the pair, allowing Miss Pryde, playing in a cute pair of pigtails, to take out the first set 6–0. Thereafter Miss Stevens, the Aucklander, came on to her form and snared the second set at 8–6. The third set was also 8–6, but this time in Miss Pryde's favour and so she collected the championship title.

Of course, young lady tennis stars were not new then nor are they exceptional today. 'Lottie' Dod won Wimbledon in 1887 as a fifteen-year-old and had won no fewer than five Wimbledons by the time she was twenty-one. Maureen ('Little Mo') Connolly captivated the world with her first United States Open at sixteen years while in recent years Tracey Austin twice captured the same title before she passed her eighteenth year. Still, a combined age of thirty-one years for two finalists at a national championship cannot, to date, be bettered.

Misses Stevens and Pryde were not lost to tennis after their 1967 teenage triumph. Under their married names Marilyn Lawrence and Anne Lee both stayed prominent in tennis, at mostly a New Zealand level, for many years after. Marilyn Pryde had her best

moment at the Benson & Hedges New Zealand Open at Stanley Street in Auckland in 1971, reaching the final only to lose to the great Australian Evonne Goolagong.

SPORTSQUOTE

Radio

One of the classics of radio's early days of sports news (bear in mind the way tennis scores used to be handwritten with a / between the games won in each set, just as shillings and pence were written, i.e., 6/3 6/2 6/1):

Announcer: 'Well, ladies and gentlemen, we have that tennis score for you now, Smith beat Brown 6 and 3, 6 and 2, 6 and a penny!'

Davis Cup Disasters

Before 1924 New Zealand tennis players appeared in the Davis Cup only as members of a composite Australasia team. In that year New Zealand broke away, but success was hardly immediate — in fact it took forty-nine years of endeavour before they recorded their first win in the second round!

New Zealand made its solo Davis Cup debut in Prague in 1924 but the newcomers were thrashed roundly 4–0 by the Czechs. Mind you, the make-up of the New Zealand team hardly inspired confidence. One of the players, F. M. B. Fisher, was aged forty-six and had served as a captain in the Boer War twenty-five years earlier. Between the years 1904 and 1914 Mr Fisher had been a member of

Parliament and had risen to a Cabinet post for three years immediately before the First World War. Fisher's New Zealand team mate was J. C. Peacock. He was of a similar age and with Fisher had won the New Zealand doubles title twenty-three years before!

Down through the years our Davis Cup team ventured to some strange locations to play the game. In 1934 they were back in Prague, as they were again in 1947. In 1957 they played in Beirut and in 1960 in Caracas, Venezuala. Non-playing captain Allan Burns remembers taking the New Zealand team to the Philippines in 1963. The home team won 3–2, to send New Zealand tumbling out of the contest for yet another year, but Burns recalls with not inconsiderable chagrin that the top Philippines player, Feliccimo Ampon, was forty-three years old and played in long trousers!

Perhaps the strangest opponent New Zealand has had in the Davis Cup was in 1975. That year the Stanley Street courts of Auckland played host to a team from South Vietnam, then a country in the throes of rebuilding after the devastation of the Vietnam War.

For the tie New Zealand put in a team that was probably the strongest we have ever fielded. Two players then both very high on world rankings, Onny Parun and Brian Fairlie, were chosen for the singles matches with the Simpson brothers, Jeffrey and Russell, the back-up players. By contrast, the Vietnamese team were all policemen, were small in stature, had no qualifications internationally and had never played on grass courts.

The three-day tie was really a farce, yet such was the thirst Auckland peo-

ple had — and still have — for top-class tennis that the stadium was full each session of play.

On day one Onny Parun took only fifty-eight minutes to beat Vo Van Tan 6–1, 6–0, 6–1, and Brian Fairlie took sixteen minutes longer in beating Ta Dui Bo 6–2, 6–2, 6–1. Hardly a game went more than four or five points. On day two the doubles lasted only sixty-two minutes as Parun and Fairlie beat Lee Min An and Din Wok Tan 6–4, 6–2, 7–5.

Came the third day and the two non-playing captains agreed that New Zealand could substitute, in the name of getting some closer matches, the Simpson brothers for Parun and Fairlie. But the hapless Vietnamese fared no better. Russell Simpson, in his first Davis Cup tie, won the first nineteen points of the day, took the first set in only fourteen minutes and the match in forty-nine minutes. Jeff Simpson had it just as easy. His opponent appeared to give up early in the match and only a few errors from Simpson Senior prolonged the match to fifty minutes.

After the tie the polite, smiling Vietnamese were given a most sympathetic reception from the crowd before disappearing into tennis oblivion again.

Parun's Hat

Each year the Benson & Hedges New Zealand Open remains one of the most friendly and hospitable tennis events for reporters and fans alike. Even though the tournament has now fallen behind other more lucrative ones on the tennis tour, it still retains its own particular and indescribable style and

Was it simply tennis skill that helped Onny Parun defeat the whole Davis Cup team of France? Or how much did the lucky white hat help? *Photograph by Ross Setford*

warmth. Some have even called it 'The Little Wimbledon of the South Pacific'.

One of the more intriguing times at the Stanley Street courts was the year the doughty New Zealander Onny Parun kept his faith in a baggy hat, beat the entire French Davis Cup team, and ended up breaking the drought for home winners in the men's singles.

This was in January 1973 and Parun was then right at the peak of his powers as a world tennis force. He had twice been to the last eight at Wimbledon and within a year was to make the Grand Prix Masters final (for the top eight players in the world) at Melbourne. He would have been mindful that not since 1959, fourteen years earlier, had a New Zealander won the men's singles of the Benson & Hedges tournament. (The 1959 winner had been Jeff Robson.)

The draw for the tournament resulted in there being Frenchmen ahead of Parun whichever way he looked. The whole French Davis Cup squad was using the Auckland tournament as a valuable work-out on grass in case they should be required to play on it during one of their future ties.

Onny Parun started by meeting the New Caledonian Bill N'Godrella in the first round. N'Godrella was, one supposes, a forerunner of Yannick Noah in the French team. Big, black and flamboyant he was. But Parun sneaked past him in a five-set thriller and went on to play the balding Georges Govern in the next round. Govern was an easier win for the New Zealander and so was Patrice Dominguez in the semifinals. That meant only Patrick Proisy lay between Parun and the title he so keenly sought, if only to prove to the New Zealand public that he could be a winner at home.

Against Proisy in the final Parun started nervously. The day was superb and the centre court at Stanley Street was packed. Parun dropped the first two sets by 4–6, 6–7. Proisy was playing well. During the next change of ends Parun dipped his hand into his courtside bag and pulled out an old battered floppy hat. Those of us who had been fortunate to have seen Parun play a lot knew that this was a special lucky charm for him. Well, his 'old faithful' did the job again.

Though there were other moments in the match when all seemed bleak for Parun, in true fighting Kiwi style he slowly wore his opponent down and finally won 4–6, 6–7, 6–2, 6–0, 7–6, after watching a Proisy lob sail over the baseline in the tenth point of the fifth set tie-breaker. Parun was a craggy character not given to excessive shows of emotion, but this day he whooped and yelled at his moment of victory and punched a spare ball high out of the stadium in triumph. The crowd loved him!

After placing his rough floppy hat carefully back in his pack, its good luck having worked for him in yet another tournament, Parun could look back on a significant win for New Zealand tennis — he had singlehandedly devoured the cream of French tennis. His day was complete when the cheque, and trophy for winning, were presented to him by the President of the Auckland Lawn Tennis Association. That year he was none other than the 1959 winner, Jeff Robson.

Host to the Aussies

If you look up an *Australian Sporting Almanack* you will notice that their national tennis championships began in 1905. Strange as it may seem, their second-ever championships were held in New Zealand. This was because of a tennis amalgamation between the two countries, which meant that the leading Australian players came to Christchurch in 1906.

In what was billed as the 'Australasian' Championships there was little luck for the Aussies at Christchurch. The young Anthony Wilding, destined to win four Wimbledon men's titles, started on his journey to tennis fame by winning the tournament. The 'Australasian' event also came to New Zealand in 1912 when it was won by the Englishman J. C. Parkes. The venue was Hastings.

SWIMMING

Gullible Gun-toter!

Was there ever a funnier moment than that which occurred at the
New Zealand swimming championships in Timaru in the early years
of the 1950s?

Picture the scene if you can. Those were the days of narrow outdoor pools with diving boards above, tin sheds for changing rooms and competitors decked out in the rather larger swimming trunk fashions of the day.

Apparently the Timaru officials were doing a fine job of organising and running the races to plan. But as they did so they did not know there was mischief afoot.

During a break in the programme, two competitors, one of whom is remembered as being the 1950 Empire Games breaststroker Trevor Eagle, went strolling on a nearby beach for relaxation. When they came across a dead seagull on the sand a scheme for some fun was planned between the two.

That night the competition restarted at the Century Pool under floodlights. The two swimmers, with the dead bird

well hidden, sneaked up the ladder of the poolside diving tower and hid above the swimmers on the diving board, in the pitchblack darkness.

Soon another heat of swimmers arrived on the blocks below for yet another race. The starter stood behind them, called them on to their starting blocks and raised his starter's gun.

At the blast of the gun the swimmers took off, while with perfect timing the dead seagull was dropped from the darkness above. Those who were there say the look on the starter's face as he gazed alternately at the dead bird at his feet and at his smoking gun will never be forgotten.

The appropriately named Mr Eagle and his anonymous friend tiptoed away to a place in New Zealand sporting history as the pullers of one of the funniest stunts ever.

Past it at Thirty-five?

The oldest New Zealander to swim at the Olympic or Commonwealth Games was Peter Mathieson. He swam at the 1950 Empire Games in Auckland at the age of thirty-five. By today's standards Peter was a veritable antique, but even so he picked up a bronze in the 3 x 110 yards medley relay, and finished fourth in the 110-yards backstroke.

Champion!

The first New Zealander to swim in the Olympic Games was Malcolm Champion. At the Stockholm games of 1912 he was a member of the four-man 4 x 200 metres relay team which splashed its way to gold. Two points of note. Champion's fellow swimmers were . . . Australians! He was a member of an Australasian squad. The time put up by the Kiwi and his Aussie comrades was 10 minutes 11.6 seconds: today's world record (set in 1992) stands at 7 minutes 11.95 seconds!

BITS AND PIECES

These modern kids may rave about Allan Hewson or Robbie Deans but was there ever an All Black goal-kicker like the great Bob Scott? Landing them from 50 yards was no problem in bare feet for this great player. *Photograph:* Evening Post

Bizarre Venues

A top ten of the weirdest and most unlikely places in which New Zealand national teams have played:

1 The 1972 New Zealand touring men's softball team played at a small island called Negros Occidental, 800 miles out to sea from the capital city of the Philippine Islands! The team's arrival gave the locals their first view of a jet plane!

2 The 1967 soccer match between New Zealand and Australia was not played, as is normal, at either Sydney, Auckland or Melbourne but instead at Saigon in war-torn South vietnam. The two teams were there for a major tournament and the match was played amid strict security. Australia won 5–3. The sound of bombs and gunfire could clearly be heard.

3 In the same vein, the 1937 New Zealand Davis Cup match against China was not played as might have been expected at any of the major New Zealand cities or at any of those exotic places of the Orient. Instead, it was played at Brighton in England!

4 The 1962 New Zealand hockey team played in the World Series in Ahmedabad, India, and stopped off on the way home for tests with Burma in Rangoon.

5 The 1978 New Zealand women's softball team played their World Series in El Salvador. And the 1974 New Zealand men's amateur golf team played their world event in the Dominican Republic.

6 With the expansion of the horizons of the New Zealand cricket team there have been some exotic ports of call for the team. The 1984 tourists visited Sri Lanka and played in Galle, a seaside resort where an ancient Portuguese castle formed one boundary line. Other venues included Radella and Moratuwa, hardly household names among cricketing locations. Later in the year a Young New Zealand team visited Zimbabwe where, among other places, they played at Kwekwe, Hwange and Mutare. Then followed a full New Zealand team's tour to Pakistan, where again there were some unlikely international cricketing venues — Sialkot, Bahawalpur and Multan.

But the place that provided the most 'hard-case' location was Berbice in Guyana which played host to the 1985 team for a one-day match against the West Indies.

Berbice is several hours' flying time inland from Georgetown in Guyana. The New Zealand and West Indies players took only a day trip to the ground. Some players travelled by small plane, others by helicopter. The airstrips were extremely primitive and so was the condition of the ground. Stones and bottles littered the outfield and the dressing room facilities were extremely modest.

As the game progressed and the New Zealand team batted, chasing the mammoth 259 for 5 scored by the West Indies players, the Kiwis who had been dismissed were ushered away to the airstrip so that the small planes could leave before the deadline for dusk flying.

In the end the only New Zealanders still at the ground were the last two batsmen, the team manager and Radio New Zealand's commentator Bryan Waddle. When the last wicket fell they too scampered to the airport. Anything to get out of Berbice, Guyana!

7 Do not forget the 1981–2 New Zealand World Cup soccer squad. They played in many places on their road to Spain. From Ba in Fiji to Beijing in China. Also the exotic cities of Riyadh, Malaga and Seville.

8 The New Zealand amateur roller skating team competed at the world champion-ships in Essen, West Germany, in 1966 and at Vicenza in Italy in 1968.

9 The rugby league 'Kiwis' tend to stay with the established cities that are the strongholds of their game, i.e. Sydney and Brisbane, the South of France and the North of England. However, at most of the grounds on which the All Blacks played in France in 1977 and 1981 the rugby league 'Kiwis' had been years before. That sort of 'doubling-up' between league and union is not per-mitted in most other countries where both sports are played. Though for the life of me I do not know why!

Anyway, I have it on good authority that the 1947-8 rugby league team on its way to Great Britain played an exhibition in Panama City.

10 Concerning the All Blacks, about the most unusual place one could say they have played is — in Bethlehem! Not, however, in the place where Christ was born. The footballers showed their gifts in Bethlehem, South Africa, in 1970. New Zealand also played a match in Uruguay in 1976, an offbeat rugby outpost. That game was significant as it marked the debuts of no fewer than thirteen All Blacks, including the great captain Graham Mourie.

Cliché!

'Rugby was the winner out there today.'

'Cricket is a funny game.'

'The horse was a certainty beaten.'

'I'll announce my retirement at the beginning of next season.'
'We had our chances out there today.'

'There was no quarter given and none asked for.'

'We'll take each game as it comes.'

(To the referee.) 'Sir, you refereed to the best of your ability.'

'Put the rent on him next start.'

And two more heard at every after-match party, year in, year out:

'I'd like our fullers (fellows) to be upstanding and drink a bumper toast to their fullers.'

'And finally I'd like to thank the ladies out the back for the spread.'

Every Dog Has its Day

True recognition has not, I feel, been given to the part the humble dog has played in the history of New Zealand sport. I therefore have decided to include a small piece on dogs to pay homage to some of the deeds they have done for (or against!) sporting people in this country!

In 1971 at the third rugby test between New Zealand and the Lions at Athletic Park in Wellington, the New Zealand centre that day was a young lad from Christchurch named Howard Joseph. Playing in only his second international he had seen New Zealand rocked back by the British backs. Barry John had opened with a dropped goal, then Gerald Davies had scored a try which John converted, then John scored himself, landed the goal and the Lions led 13–0 at half time.

I mention the scoring in detail to make the point that in the second half New Zealand was desperate for points to save the game. Slowly more ball began to come the way of the All Black backs. Finally a good running situation was reached and the ball passed through the hands of Sid Going at

halfback and out to the backs. As Cottrell, Duncan and Joseph lined up, the crowd sensed that here at last was the chance New Zealand had been waiting for to strike back at the big British lead. But no! Who pulled off the stunning leg-trip on Joseph that ruined the day? Not Williams or Duckham or Dawes of the Lions but a smallish brown dog, of indiscriminate parentage, who had decided to stray on to the field and play his part. The movement broke down without a score, the match was lost and, while it would be wrong to lay the whole blame on the dog, Howard Joseph was never seen on the field for his country after that match. Nowhere in my deep research of this event is there comment on what Joseph said at the moment of impact between dog and man. Nor is there a record of what happened to the dog!

All that remains is TV coverage of the game with Cliff Morgan commentating, 'Here's the ball with the New Zealand backs,' Morgan says on the soundtrack. 'Going has it . . . Cottrell . . . Joseph . . . he's fallen over a dog,' and then on Morgan goes without so

No wonder the pace looks brisk here in the 1950 Empire Games marathon. The small dog followed this group of runners for several kilometres and later did his bit to upset the eventual winner, Jack Holden of England.

much as a patriotic thank you to the canine defender who saved the day.

Mind you, some dogs in New Zealand's sporting history have not been as treacherous to their own country as was the Wellington one that day in 1971. In 1950 during the marathon at the Empire Games in Auckland two dogs ran alongside and did their best to distract Jack Holden, the forty-three-year-old Englishman, who was on his way to the gold medal.

First, there was a small black-and-white dog who ran in and about Holden's feet for about three kilometres. In the rainy conditions Holden eventually discarded his shoes and ran the last eleven kilometres in bare feet. He outpaced the little dog but soon the slap of his feet on the wet streets attracted the attention of a second dog. This was the Kiwi secret weapon. He leapt and barked and jumped about

playfully in a definite attempt to trip up the English-man. To no avail, however. Holden was upset by the dog, and cursed him several times, but soon ran on to his victory circuit of Eden Park leaving the brave (and patriotic) New Zealand dogs behind.

Another case of a dog affecting the outcome of a major sporting event came with the running of the 1920 Great Northern Steeplechase at Ellerslie in Auckland. This race has been called the severest test of a steeplechase horse in the southern hemisphere. Three times they have to journey up Ellerslie's notorious hill during a race of twenty-five jumps.

In the Great Northern of 1920 a horse called Garryowen was well clear of his rivals when he approached the fence on top of the hill for the last time. Having cleared it with ease it was fully expected that he would run on down the hill and win comfortably. But there was a dog among a group of spectators at the top of the hill. When the horses passed, the dog broke away from the throng and set off after Garryowen. The poor horse toppled over the dog and fell. Much to the horror of horse-lovers, but not, one presumes, of punters who had backed others in the field, Garryowen broke a leg and had to be destroyed. Again my research gives me no details on the dog and what happened to him. Was he taken by the backers of the eventual winner to a butcher's shop and fed on only the best steaks? I guess one will never know.

It seems many New Zealand sports clubs adopt a dog to act as a deterrent to intruders breaking in while the clubhouse is empty. Many are the rugby fans who changed their minds about showing a friend over Lancaster Park, mostly because of the huge German shepherd who stalked about when the groundsman was absent.

One of the clubs that fell in love with a dog was the Eastbourne Bowling Club near Wellington. According to an issue of the *New Zealand Sportsman* in December 1947, when their dog Chum died his photograph was hung in the Eastbourne clubhouse in much the same way as illustrious past members' portraits are.

Chum was owned by a Mr Leo Cimino. While Leo played bowls the dog also bowled. The players would give Chum a bowl of his own which he would nudge with his nose along the bank by the side of the green. Should the bowl fall into the ditch the dog would never dream of stepping on to the green to possibly upset his master's game. Instead he would wait patiently for one of the players to replace his bowl on the bank so he could continue with his game. When Chum died he was buried in the grounds of the club near the big tree that was his resting spot after the rigours of a long match.

Coming into the era of live television, the first dog I can recall making his mark was a big brown setter who

This canine cricket fan chose his moment well. There was live radio and television coverage at the time of his appearance on Eden Park in Auckland during the 1984 cricket test between New Zealand and England. Famous players watch and wait as two officials chase the offender from the pitch. Later, the players had to help. *Photograph:* Auckland Star

117

followed a televised track race at Newtown Park in Wellington. The dog was so beautifully graceful as he bounded beside the puffing athletes no one could be really angry with him. Then there was the time at Lancaster Park that a tiny corgi shuffled on to the pitch during the Lions versus Canterbury match of 1977. Several players approached him inviting him to leave but he neatly sidestepped them all. Alex Wyllie, the grizzly Canterbury captain, introduced the farmer's touch by creeping towards the intruder making the whistling and kissing noises one does to a friendly dog. Meanwhile, the touch judge stole up behind him (the dog that is, not Wyllie) and hustled the wee fellow away. The corgi was so enraged that his moment of glory had been prematurely ended that he bit the touch judge on the hand, an act clearly seen on television. For that act corgi was not even sent to the sin-bin!

Perhaps because they took place in more recent times two other doggy stories come to mind. In 1984 during the cricket test at Eden Park in Auckland between New Zealand and England a pacey Doberman pinscher wandered on to the ground. This time Jeremy Coney assumed the role of dog catcher, but the big dog merely lolloped away and dashed about outfield showing commendable speed. The game was held up for about six minutes in what was a very good attempt to disrupt the concentration of the English batsmen. Eventually the New Zealand players, in a splendid herding movement that they must have practised and that would have done a sheepdog trial proud, showed the dog the gate. When there was nowhere else to go, the dog,

realising that his distracting work was done, bolted through the gate to the roar of 20,000 throats. His little place in sporting history was secure.

Actually, that dog at Eden Park was good for New Zealand sport in many ways. First, his presence induced the funniest piece of radio commentary heard in this country for many a year (delivered by the BBC's Don Mosey). Secondly, he became the first dog ever to be subjected to a slow-motion television replay. The rush through the gate chased by the players made even better viewing second time around! The dog's day was made, and his job was done for his country, when David Gower was dismissed soon after!

My last story about dogs reports a disturbing drop in standards. This one came from the 1984 Shell Cup cricket final between Auckland and Wellington at the Basin Reserve in Wellington. Halfway through the afternoon a black dog, again of doubtful breeding, wandered on to the field. Play in the game stopped while the umpires and several players made moves towards him. However, he was hell-bent on leaving his mark on the day. Proceeding to a place directly in front of the hallowed R. A. Vance grandstand (the finest in the land, I might add), the dog proceeded to disgrace himself thoroughly on the turf. That having been done he scuffed disdainfully at the grass and trotted off. They do say crowd behaviour at cricket has slipped in recent years. This disturbing trend seems to be affecting the dogs too.

In the Family

In the modern age of swift travel between countries several New

Zealand families have achieved prominence, for more than the country of their birth, at the Olympic or Commonwealth Games.

In 1962 at Perth in the Empire Games Bob Binning of Hawke's Bay was entered in four events at his sport of fencing. Along with Brian Pickworth and Mike Henderson he was successful in winning a medal in one of those events — the team sabre. Binning took home a silver medal to show to his family and friends in Hastings. He also competed in the 1966 Commonwealth Games at Kingston, but just missed out on the medals there.

Presumably all this sporting prowess was inspirational to Bob Binning's daughter Ricki because, on reaching her teens, she was showing through as a swimmer of exceptional talent. New Zealand titles came her way and soon she was on the brink of Olympic and Commonwealth Games selection. But Ricki chose Australia as the country of her sporting destiny. Leaving New Zealand early in the 1980s, she settled in Australia and made Australian rankings. Her times were so good that she was selected for the world championships and the Brisbane Commonwealth Games. She swam in several finals at Brisbane.

Another New Zealand family has produced international sportsmen at home and in Australia. The Rowe family of Christchurch had their daughter Lynne swimming for New Zealand at the 1976 Olympics in Montreal. Their son Paul made the New Zealand swim team for Edmonton two years later and was also picked for the Moscow Olympics of 1980. But between 1980 and 1982 Paul set off for the sterner competition of Australia and in what

seemed like no time at all he was competing against New Zealanders for his adopted country. Paul won a gold medal for Australia at the 4 x 200-metre relay and a silver in the 200-metre butterfly.

There are several examples of sportsmen winning medals for New Zealand as well as for other countries at the Commonwealth Games. Precious McKenzie is one (in flyweight weightlifting for Great Britain as well), Morgan Moffat the Scottish bowler is another (for Scotland at Christchurch, a bronze medal; for New Zealand at Edmonton and Brisbane, a silver medal at each).

But to my knowledge the fencer Melody ('Dot') Gard (nee Coleman) is the only New Zealand woman to win a medal for another country at an Olympic or Commonwealth Games as well as for New Zealand. As Dot Coleman she won the first gold medal awarded at the Empire games in Perth 1962. Then she represented Australia at the Kingston Games of 1966 and won a silver in the women's team foil competition.

Mixing It

When did the New Zealand rugby league team play three official tour matches under rugby union rules? When did the MCC cricket team play a proper soccer match on Wellington's hallowed rugby turf at Athletic Park? When, indeed, did the All Blacks play in the Chatham Cup soccer competition? And when did the All Blacks take part in a most serious squash international? To some of the above questions there are exceptional and novel cir-

The All Golds thirteen which, under Rugby Union rules, met and defeated at Sydney, on August 17, 1907, by 11—8, the first Kangaroos. The visitors won the three matches played prior to embarking on their historic pioneer tour of England.

cumstances to be sure. But others were deadly serious.

Back in 1907 the rock that was the game of rugby union's solid base in New Zealand was shaken to its very core by the formation of a breakaway game, then called Northern Union, to be later known as rugby league. The move arose from a feeling among the players that they should receive some financial reward for best efforts, but the rules of the time stated, as they still do today, that no person in rugby union could be paid for playing the game. Therefore, the disgruntled players of 1907 broke away to form a new professional game. Such were the beginnings of rugby league in New Zealand.

Acting on the advice of members of the famous 1905–6 All Blacks, a Mr A.

H. Baskerville formed a professional New Zealand team and arranged for them a tour to Great Britain. The team of pioneers left New Zealand in 1907 *en route* to their new sporting destiny. By boat they journeyed across the Tasman Sea and stopped in Sydney. There they attracted the interest of rugby footballers in Sydney who challenged them to a game or two during their boat's stay.

The New Zealanders had never seen the Northern Union game played (they actually purchased a rule book to study before the tour started), so although they welcomed the chance of playing football, they wished not unnaturally to play under rules with which they were familiar. Thus it came about that a New Zealand rugby league team played an Australian rugby union team in three matches under rugby union laws.

As the New Zealand team contained four members of the 1905–6 All Blacks (George Smith, Duncan McGregor, 'Massa' Johnston and William Mackrell) plus others who had been All Blacks before that, and twenty players in all who had played to representative standard in 1907 at rugby union, the Australian players knew they were in for a tough time. In all there were three games played during this little-remembered series and in each New Zealand beat the Australians, the scores being 11–8, 19–5 and 5–3. Over 42,000 people paid to see the three games.

The New Zealand team was so impressed by one of the Australians, H. H. 'Dally' Messenger, that he was invited to tour Great Britain with the Kiwi party. Messenger became one of the stars of the touring team.

When they returned home a year later having won eighteen of thirty-four games in Britain, Messenger introduced Australians to the new game, which today thrives in New South Wales and Queensland. The New Zealanders, nicknamed the 'All Golds' because they had dared to play for cash, came home to New Zealand and rugby league flourished as a result of their success on tour.

The occasion the MCC cricket team played soccer on Athletic Park was equally as serious as the 'All Golds' on tour. It was in the same year, 1907, when the first MCC team had fulfilled its cricketing obligations to its New Zealand hosts. On Wednesday 13 March a game of soccer was arranged for the touring cricketers against a

Wellington team. Within the MCC team's ranks were a number of excellent football exponents. Three were Cambridge Blues and one was from Oxford, while others had experience of amateur-club play in England. The end result, a 5–0 win to England, was hailed by the *New Zealand Mail* as 'as fine an exhibition of soccer football as had been seen by the best English teams'.

What with the defection of a stack of its leading players to rugby league and cricketers playing soccer on Athletic Park, rugby union officials must have been a bewildered lot in 1907!

The case of an English cricket team playing soccer was not a oncer. The situation was repeated in March 1936 when the MCC team defeated a full Wellington representative soccer side 5–2 at the Basin Reserve. The Hon. C. J. Lyttelton played fullback for the MCC. He was later the very popular Governor-General, Lord Cobham, and was still good enough to hit a massive six out of Eden Park in a special cricket match in his honour in 1961.

With regard to the All Blacks almost winning the Chatham Cup, here is where the author enjoys a little licence. For those with short memories the Chatham Cup was for fifty years

The New Zealand Press squash team which played the All Blacks rugby team while on tour in South Africa in 1976. *Back row from left* Ross Wiggins (*New Zealand Herald*), Bob Howitt (*Rugby News*) Paul Cavanaugh (NZ Press Association), Keith Quinn (Television New Zealand), John Howson (Radio New Zealand) Front row Co-opted South African journalists Gerhard Burger and Rory Brown. The confident smiles were not matched by the results. The All Blacks won 4–2.

the New Zealand equivalent of the English FA Cup and many were the soccer clubs from north and south who strove to win the trophy.

The All Blacks to whom I refer were in fact nothing to do with the game of rugby. They were the Millerton All Blacks from the soccer outcrop of Buller. The tiny town of Millerton, with its team dressed in black, made the final of the Chatham Cup twice. In 1932 the Millerton All Blacks lost 5–1 to the Marist Club of Wellington while in 1933 Ponsonby of Auckland beat them 2–1.

Allow your author more bending of the facts in the case of the All Blacks' 'international' against a top-class squash team. This came on the 1976 tour of South Africa when the tour had

reached Bloemfontein between the third and fourth tests.

Along the way on that trip many of the players had made regular use of the superb squash facilities that they found at the plush sporting clubs at which they trained. The touring journalists enjoyed similar advantages and soon a rivalry built up between the two groups.

Eventually the challenge of a squash test was laid and accepted, bets were wagered, and two teams of six apiece were drawn from the touring media and the All Blacks.

For the sake of historical exactness I can record that the All Blacks caused something of a sensation when their selection panel dropped the team's rugby coach, John ('J.J.') Stewart.

Without him the All Blacks' line-up was still strong and they eventually beat the reporters by 4 matches to 2. I can also record, for sporting history, that the author suffered a straight sets defeat at the hands of that deft left-hander Doug Bruce.

But by far the best match of the series was a torrid five-setter between All Black Kerry Tanner and Radio New Zealand reporter John Howson. For the life of me I had better not reveal the result, except to say that, at the completion of the last point, over 400 rand changed hands, such was the heavy betting on both champs!

Sports Reporters

Sports reporters can be a canny lot at times. Take this example from Radio New Zealand's popular Wellington sportscaster Colin McKenzie: A few years ago McKenzie was the RHNZ touring correspondent with the New Zealand rugby league team in Australia. One day on tour he filed a report home that not only told his listeners what had happened that day to the Kiwis but also told those who listened just that little bit closer how he, personally, had fared that day.

McKenzie said this on radio in his report:

'Today the Kiwi rugby league team flew from Sydney to Brisbane, arriving in mid-afternoon after some slight travel hitches along the way. When the touring group of thirty-five players and pressmen arrived at Sydney Airport it was found that there were only thrity-four seats booked on the flight. So one of the reporters was asked by the team management to stay behind at Sydney Airport. This is Colin McKenzie . . . at Sydney Airport!'

It's the kind of instinctive cleverness that can make the great sports report, which I believe that one was.

One of the difficulties of making a report for a radio station or newspaper is the tight strictures of the final deadline. The need to file one's copy exactly on time can force a reporter to race through his writing under pressure and therefore run the risk of making errors, etc.

This never used to worry Christchurch's Cyril Walter, who for years coached and wrote on the sport of hockey in that city. *There* was a man who knew his subject to a depth and breadth that few, if any, have ever matched and never bettered in New Zealand.

The problem of deadlines never bothered Cyril Walter. Quite simply, he used to rise on a Saturday morning, gather his thoughts and write the reports of the games he was to watch later that afternoon! Of course, he would leave spaces for an opening paragraph that detailed the full-time score and scorers and he sometimes added a summary sentence or two but basically when he arrived at the local hockey ground to watch his assigned games he already had his report tucked away in his back pocket!

At least you could say that Cyril attended the matches he was supposed to. One Australian sports reporter a few years back filed live radio summaries from New Zealand back to Australia on a game he never actually saw.

This also was to do with the sport of rugby league. The Australian reporter, it seemed, was having a whale of a tour of New Zealand and, not to put too fine a point on it, had made a strong acquaintance with a young local woman while on that tour.

When the team he was assigned to follow arrived at Wellington his office at home in Sydney did not, it seemed, rate the match there as being worthy enough for a full radio commentary description. So the reporter was merely asked to file four telephone reports during the floodlit game. So, being keen on the young woman in question and not wanting to miss out on the chance of perhaps a nice dinner with her on a cold Wellington night, our intrepid Australian enlisted the help of a local reporter.

'Can you, mate,' he asked of the youngster, 'phone me in my hotel room four times in the match with what's happening out there at the ground?' For a slight monetary exchange the local fellow agreed.

In the evening that followed, the Aussie's candlelit dinner in his hotel room with the young woman was, presumably, a most agreeable occasion interrupted only four times by the phone ringing.

Sure enough, each time the caller was the local reporter fulfilling his side of the deal and telling the story of what was happening out at the park. The Aussie listened, made notes, replaced the receiver and then phoned direct to his home station in Sydney. Minutes later, live on the air, he then repeated the match score and information, embellishing things with verbal intonations as he might do if he was actually at the ground himself! After each call his station thanked him and asked him to call again in twenty mintues. No one was any the wiser!

Mock-Up

False or mocked-up commentaries are part and parcel of radio and television.

The best known of the fake commentaries in New Zealand occurred on the 1953–4 New Zealand cricket tour of South Africa. In those days the cost of having broadcasts come in on radio for long periods of time was prohibitive and there were enormous problems with the quality of the broadcasts. It was obvious that an alternative system was needed, otherwise the test matches would not be heard.

The method that was adopted by the New Zealand broadcasting authorities of the time was a copy of one that had been used successfully by Australia when they had found that they could not 'hear' their cricket teams playing in England.

Instead of hearing commentary from the ground, telegrams were cabled in an abbreviated form from South Africa to New Zealand. These were sent at the end of each over in a special code that the senders and receivers understood. Each telegram gave details of each ball bowled in the previous over, who bowled to whom, where each ball was hit to on the field, who fielded it and how many runs might have been scored. The telegrams would have made no sense to anyone but those who waited at the other end and who knew the code.

The 'commentators' sat in the studio in New Zealand and on receipt of each telegram they then adlibbed a full description of the play interpreting the code. These commentaries were exactly like a live match. They had all the usual cricketing asides and comments. There might be long dissertations about the New Zealand batsmen or the bowling attack or how they were toiling away in the particular weather description that had been previously sent. Information was added about the field placings as the coded figures matched with numbers on squares marked on a map of the ground. Comments were made about quite descriptive things like the wind blowing the flags on top of the grandstands or the applause for a player when he had reached his century. Indeed, sound effects were added in from a local library of tapes and records. The distinctive sound of the cricket ball hitting the bat was created by tapping a desktop with a piece of stick or a large pencil.

The whole operation was rated a huge success and many people listening in did not know it was all make believe!

In Great Form

A few years ago TVNZ's management decided to send Phillip Leishman, their usual race presenter, to the Melbourne Cup. His assignment was to report especially on what was happening to the New Zealand horses, jockeys and trainers.

Being a diligent sort of a chap, Leishman made sure he was totally prepared as he headed out to the Flemington track on race day. There he made contact with the local TV technical staff who ushered him to a commentary place that was clearly marked 'TVNZ'. A young man from the local station was deputed to sit with him for technical assistance.

Leishman spread his copious notes out at his commentary position and then he and the technical man sat waiting for the crossover from New Zealand. It was a big day for the young New Zealand broadcaster and he felt

he was ready to do a good job for the viewers back home.

At about the same time in New Zealand, at the traditional hour in the later afternoon the Melbourne Cup telecast started. But when the New Zealand studio frontman, working out of the Avalon studios in Lower Hutt, crossed to 'our man Phillip Leishman in Melbourne', nothing happened. Instead, the Australian presentation came on. There was obviously a difficulty in getting the New Zealand commentary position on to the air.

The Aussie broadcasters, as is their style, were doing a good job, though what they were saying was not directly slanted towards New Zealand. But as TVNZ's technical staff could not raise a peep from Flemington and therefore could not get Leishman's call on air it was eventually presumed that, for some reason, he was not at the track. Therefore TVNZ decided to stay with the description they were receiving from the Australian broadcasters. It was, after all, a live telecast and in a crisis you take what you get.

Meanwhile at Flemington, Leishman remembers how surprised he was, then slightly annoyed at the late crossover time he was obviously going to receive from the Avalon studios in New Zealand. In impatience he finally asked the technician who was sitting next to him whether he was 'on' or not. The technical man, also wearing headphones, appeared to listen intently on them for a moment and then with a flourish pointed vigorously at the New Zealander in the time-honoured tradition of, 'Cue, go, you're on now!' Leishman, understanding at last that he was on the air, launched into his broadcast. As he relates the story years later, he tells of how all his pre-race preparation paid off. Every shot the Australian TV director put up on screen he was able to match with flawless new information, news and comment and it all, as TVNZ had wanted, was angled to the New Zealand audience watching across the Tasman.

'I was,' says Phillip, these days remembering his own performance, 'in great form.'

The race came and went and the great occasion of the Melbourne Cup was as exciting and colourful as ever. After the actual race call and all the thrill of seeing the Cup field of the best horses in Australasia turn for home and find its winner Leishman, from his vantage point high in the Flemington grandstand, waxed lyrical one more time, calling on his great descriptive powers to summarise what had been a great afternoon. He then wrapped up his broadcast and in another time-honoured tradition, crossed back to the studios in New Zealand.

A greatly relieved Leishman then took off his microphone and headset, his day's work being over. Casually, he asked the Australian technician, still sitting with him, how his work had gone down with his New Zealand colleagues back home.

'Bewdy,' replied the technician, bustling about unplugging plugs etc.

Phillip Leishman never saw that man again. Which was a shame as he later would have wanted to ask him several questions.

The New Zealander then returned to his hotel and prepared to take a couple of days of annual leave in Australia before returning home, via Christchurch, where his parents, Dave and Noeline Leishman from Timaru, were on hand to greet him. By then it was over a week since the Cup day and the subject of the race was hardly top of the list for Leishman as he greeted his mother and father. It wasn't until sometime later that he casually enquired as to whether they had enjoyed his Cup day call on TV.

'What are you talking about?' replied his mother. And the whole sad story of TVNZ being unable to make contact with the course at Flemington came out.

In the end it seems Phillip Leishman's opinion of his own broadcast from Melbourne will never be tested. For history's sake and because he is an honest man we will have to take his word that he was 'in great form' at the microphone during his forty minutes or so on air.

The facts are that he believed he broadcast the Cup after the technical man next to him made the 'go' gesture to get him started. But it may well be that those two men, Leishman and the technical fellow (plus the gremlins who prevented any of it being heard in New Zealand at any stage) were the only people (or creatures!) in the world who heard his call that day.

Caught Out

Radio New Zealand sports staff on duty in Wellington in September 1986 received a call from Paul Martin, their regular London correspondent. He wished to file with them a series of voice-pieces about the sports news of the day in Great Britain.

Calls from Martin were then a regular feature of an office day for the RNZ staffers as he was a most diligent reporter. But on this day he was caught out as being perhaps too diligent for his own good.

Martin sent from London a story about the Commonwealth Games bowls gold medallist Ian Dickison of Dunedin. Martin reported that Dickison had been playing the 'game of his life' against the top British professional and former Games winner, David Bryant.

Martin reported that the match between Dickison and Bryant had won itself a big following in Great Britain as it had been seen on television right across the country. And Martin announced with controlled elation that Dickison had been the winner, and he rated it as a significant victory for the New Zealander.

The Radio New Zealand sports staff duly ran the story in one of its early morning sports bulletins which, as any loyal listener can tell you, can be heard on literally dozens of stations from north to south.

One of those stations is 4ZB in Dunedin, Dickison's home town. The local radio sports reporter Steve Davey rose from his bed that day and was puzzled to hear this latest news as he was sure he had greeted Dickison in the street in Dunedin just two days before!

Surely, thought Davey, Dickison could not have made it to the great Wembley Arena in London in such a short space of time.

Davey rang through to Wellington where his colleagues confirmed that the report had come from Paul Martin in London and that it had arrived just that day. Nevertheless, the duty reporter felt bound to check back with Martin who, on receiving the call, said he too would check up with the BBC as he had definitely watched the game on television that afternoon and indeed had been totally engrossed by the battle.

It was a rather chastened Paul Martin who rang Radio New Zealand back a few minutes later to say that he had indeed watched the match on BBC television but after a quick check he had been told that the game had been recorded and in fact had been played four months before!

Very Keen

One of my favourite news media stories concerns commentator Peter Williams when he was a cub reporter on the Christchurch radio station 3ZB.

The young Williams was very keen and whatever he was asked to do by his bosses he pursued with a zeal and commitment that was total and which led to his later career as one of TVNZ's top commentators and frontmen.

One day his boss reminded his new protégé of a great lesson in life. 'You should always make a visitor welcome in your place,' intoned the boss, 'because you never know how grateful you will be in return one day when someone is kind to you when you are far from home.'

It was an admirable sentiment, well taken on board by the young Williams.

So when the Korean Davis Cup tennis team arrived in the Garden City to play New Zealand, the boss reminded Williams of this and dispatched him to Wilding Park to watch the visitors practising.

Once at the Park Williams scanned the stadium. The players and managers seemed happy enough in each other's company and anyway you don't interrupt international sportsmen in training. It's not done.

But a wave of sympathy swept over young Peter as he turned his attention up to the press area of the grandstand. There, sitting by himself at a typewriter, was an Asian gentleman.

To young Williams this was his chance. With the noble words of his boss ringing in his ears Williams walked up the stairs and approached the Asian-looking gentleman.

Language was going to be a problem so on speaking Williams slowed down a pace and e-nun-ci-at-ed every sylllable slowly. The Asian man looked up, looked interested, and was obviously listening.

'Good morning,' said the keen New Zealander, speaking with great clarity, 'Welcome to my city. I bring you greetings and I wish to tell you that I can help you with anything you want while you are in this town. Please feel free to ask me for help while you are here.'

The Asian gentleman broke into a wide grin and spoke for the first time.

'Gee thanks, mate,' he said. 'Pleased to meet you too. I'm Eddie Kwok of the *New Zealand Herald!*'

You Won't Believe This!

This story ran in *The Press* one day in October of 1986.

A Christchurch schoolgirl had more than just a red face after an embarrassing experience on the snowy slopes of the Mount Hutt ski-field.

She was at the top of a run with some fellow students when she felt an urgent call of nature. There was no alternative but for the other girls to form a discreet circle while she answered the call, still on skis.

But, to her horror, she began to slide forward, bursting through the human circle and down the slope, still squatting and, no doubt, screaming. Her descent stopped only when she lurched sideways, wrenching a knee.

The Mountain Rescue people swiftly made her comfortable in the first-aid room. There she was joined by a male skier who had just broken a leg.

'You won't believe this,' he told the girl. 'I was making a run when I saw this bird scooting down the slope with her pants down. I couldn't take my eyes off the sight — that's why I hit the bloody rock!'

Slips!

This newspaper quote will be published without comment. It comes from the *Southland Times Sportsview* of 13 September 1985. The paper was commenting on a broadcast gaffe by Radio New Zealand's local rugby broadcaster. The paper tried to explain the malapropism that had slipped out during the live broadcast the previous Saturday.

'Hope,' said the paper, 'muddled his words a bit when describing some furious rucking.'

Malaprops are not always the domain of a radio broadcaster but they have certainly come up with a few of the classics.

Take this example from the Pukekohe motor races a few years back. When describing how many cars were to be in the next race the local radio man traversed a rocky path.

With all seriousness he announced, 'In this race eighteen cars will stace the farter.'

Question: *There were some nervous moments for the organising committee of the Christchurch Commonwealth Games when they put their city's case to the Commonwealth Games Association. The Games of 1974 were eventually awarded to Christchurch, but which city did they have to beat in the final vote?*

Answer: *Melbourne, Australia. The final voting favoured Christchurch by 36 votes to 2.*

Policeman Extraordinary

One of my favourite characters of New Zealand sport is now-retired Detective-Inspector John ('Spike') Hughes of Auckland. For many years he fought crime with a zeal that marked him as one of the toughest and best cops in the country. At the same time, with remarkable determination and tenacity, he also maintained a sporting career that saw him reach the top level in three separate and entirely different types of recreational activity.

In his younger days, while still in the Navy, Hughes won three New Zealand amateur boxing titles in the middleweight division. He won the reputation of a fighter who would never give up until he had caught his man, an attribute that many a criminal was to rue in later years.

Hughes' superb fitness and athleticism soon carried him from boxing to the sport of squash where he quickly climbed to a top standard around Auckland's clubs, again a feared opponent because he would still be on his feet when others were exhausted.

Again after a few years the thirst to vary his sports took Hughes into marathon running and soon he gained fame as an 'ultra' man, capable of running enormous mile-ages oblivious to the body's pain barrier.

John Hughes set records at many ultra events in both New Zealand and Australia. He was, and is, enormously respected as a sportsman. He was also greatly respected as a detective, not least by the criminal element of New Zealand. From the dozens of stories about John Hughes there are a couple that spring to mind.

At one time he was preparing to run a marathon. His training had gone well and he had built up his stamina for a good run and perhaps a good time. On the day before the race Hughes eased up on his training, wishing to conserve energy so that he could give maximum effort on race day. But twenty-four hours before the start, cruising the streets in his car in his role as city policeman, he recognised among the strollers a man wanted for passing bad cheques.

Hughes did not really desire a chase so close to race day so he called out from his car and suggested the man might give himself up. The wanted man was having none of that. He took to his scrapers and the reluctant Hughes was forced to alight from his car and give chase in street clothes. Our policeman conceded quite a start to the flying fugitive who himself showed a nifty turn of speed. Up and down streets they ran, around a house several times, and over a high wall

129

before Hughes' determination to succeed eventually saw him win the chase and down his quarry with a superb tackle.

The satisfaction Hughes gained from catching his man was tempered only by having used up so much of his carefully stored physical resources, needed for the race next day.

Initiative is another quality often displayed by John Hughes. He served for a time as a radio and television boxing commentator, and one night the broadcast had scarcely started when he rose from his broadcasting seat and walked quickly to the side of the hall where he spoke quietly to a watching constable. The young constable nodded to another policeman further down the hall as Hughes resumed his seat and clipped on his microphone to continue his between-round radio commentary.

While the attention of the crowd was centred on the action in the ring the two policemen moved in, quietly asked a man to leave his seat and led him away to be charged at the police station. The gentleman concerned, peacefully watching the fistic action, was wanted for some crime. Hughes had spotted him from the broadcast position.

Then, on the night of the infamous bout at Ponsonby in 1978 when a professional boxer lashed out and kicked his opponent and punched the referee, John Hughes was involved in the live television commentary. As the irate young boxer who had perpetrated the shameful deed was led away (to be later banned for life), some of his mates decided to mix things up some more. A fellow with a wild stare in his eyes climbed the steps to the ring and made menacing gestures at those lead-

ing away his disgraced pal. John Hughes simply unhooked his microphone and stepped into the fray. He hauled away the intruder and was back in time to offer a summarising commentary for television on the whole shameful affair!

All Black Double

In the 1920s and 1930s New Zealand was very much a nation of rugby and cricket players. To succeed at both sports was therefore a double achievement of distinction. One man who made it as a 'double All Black', i.e., a national representative of rugby and cricket, was Bill Carson, originally from Gisborne, later from Auckland.

Carson was a tall, sturdy young man, standing six foot tall and weighing over fourteen stone who soon emerged as a rugby flanker of enormous potential, gaining selection for Auckland in his twentieth year after only five games of senior club play. That was in 1936 and Carson completed a notable year by later being chosen as an attacking left-hand batsman and right-hand bowler for the Auckland Plunket Shield cricket team.

In his second match in first-class cricket, at Dunedin on 31 December 1936, Carson partnered Paul Whitelaw to a world-record partnership of 445 for the third wicket, a fantastic effort by the pair, especially when one considers that the previous best had been set at 389 runs by that great Australian pair Stan McCabe and Bill Ponsford in a match against MCC at Lord's in 1934. Carson's personal tally

Carson *(left and insert)* and Paul Whitelaw pose in front of the scoreboard that records their fabulous world record for a third wicket partnership, set on New Year's Eve, 1936. Theirs stood as world record for 39 years.

was 290 runs, made in only 268 minutes! A week later he scored 259 not out for his club Eden in the Auckland Club championship. Later still in that season Carson flayed the Wellington attack for 194 runs in 124 minutes.

Such form carried him straight into the New Zealand touring team for the 1937 tour of England. While on that tour he naturally missed the New Zealand winter but in 1938 resumed his rugby in better form than ever. His Ponsonby clubmates were delighted when he was made an All Black to tour Australia under captain 'Brushy' Mitchell.

Thus Carson had achieved his double international honours by the age of twenty-two.

Bill Carson lost his life in the Second World War. An outstanding soldier, he served with distinction in Greece, Crete, Egypt, Libya, Tunisia and Italy, and in 1943 was awarded the Military Cross at the battle of Mareth. He died as a result of wounds on 8 October 1944 and was buried in the Heliopolis Military Cemetery in Egypt.

Most sporting observers of the time call him one of the outstanding young New Zealand sportsmen of his time. His cricketing career continued right up until his departure for the war zones of the Mediterranean, and he was considered a certainty for the All Black team which was originally scheduled to tour South Africa in 1940.

Question: *Who is the only man who has been chosen to represent New Zealand at an Olympic or Common wealth Games in two sports (not different events within the same sport but different sports)?*

Answer: *Les Mills, at the Commonwealth Games in 1966 in Kingston, Jamaica. Mills competed in the discus and shotput events in track and field competition, but was also chosen as a heavyweight weightlifter. Mills had great success in the two field events, winning the discus and coming second in the shot. But a strained groin injury, sustained during the discus throw, forced him to withdraw from the weightlifting. Nevertheless, still a great and unusual achievement. These days, Les Mills is the Mayor of Auckland.*

The Natives

It is often said that the best should be left till last. I had that in mind when I planned this last story in this collection of some of the more bizarre and unusual stories from New Zealand's colourful sporting history.

This time though I seek your indulgence to expand more and amplify the details more than has been the usual style in the other parts to this book. The reason is that I would really like to tell you more about my most favourite sports team from New Zealand. Their story is such an intermingling of the strange, singular and whimsical that they deserve a chapter of their own.

The team of which I write is the rugby group from this country who, in 1888 and under the name of the New Zealand Native Football Team, set sail for Australia on the first part of a tour that was to see them eventually travel once around the whole world. Their epic journey set the standard for every footballing tour that has followed down through the years. While it's true that any rugby or sporting team of today can claim to have had 'a great time' at the end of their particular weekend tour or international experience, it can be ventured with every confidence that no team ever had the total experience of life itself that the pioneering Native team enjoyed.

This was the tour of all tours. After having been lucky enough to have experienced rugby journeys of modern times, aided by jet travel, luxury accommodation and expense accounts, the 1888 Native tour is the one I would have dearly loved to have lived through.

Mind you, I am not sure what my dear wife would have said, for while I write of the 1888 Native team from New Zealand I should really be saying 1888–9 team for their voyage into the rugby unknown lasted from one year into the next. In fact, from the time they played their first tour game until the time of their last, fourteen months

of history passed them, and the world, by. One is left only to shudder at what the wives of today's well-travelled All Blacks might say to a similar venture!

But let me please go back to the start of this journey for every inch of it is worth savouring.

Brain-child

The tour was the brain-child of an Englishman, Mr Tom Eyton, who lived in New Zealand and who had been part of some of the earliest rugby played in the new Dominion (twenty-aside matches involving the Armed Constabulary near Wanganui).

Eyton fancied himself as an entrepreneur, so while he was back in England on a private visit in 1887 he watched the rugby of the day being played and thought how intriguing it might be if a team of New Zealanders could be persuaded to travel, to test the game and themselves against players from the home of rugby.

He approached the Rugby Union that organised the game in England and sought their approval. Of course such an idea was silly to their ears for a time. The thought of colonials from faraway New Zealand returning to show Englishmen themselves how to play an English game was just too absurd.

Eyton insisted he could muster a team of talent. The English officials then became suspicious of this visitor who claimed so much with so little evidence. The Rugby Football Union became distrustful of Eyton and only reluctantly agreed to sanction his planned tour provided satisfactory evidence and guarantees could be offered by Eyton as to the amateur status of the players.

Eyton knew that this was not a problem. Rugby in New Zealand at the time was a rugged, disjointed provincial game without a parent or controlling body that was unified or stable. It was certainly not a game in which one made money.

So Eyton returned to New Zealand with the idea forming in his mind of a team of Maori players making the tour. He could see that approach as a crowd-puller. To the British, all rugby players were white and sometimes well-bred from the upper classes. Their image of native New Zealanders was that of grass-skirted South Sea warriors running about with spears and tattooed faces. There was no concept of Maori as rugby players.

On his return to New Zealand Eyton set about the task of finding a team of Maori who would have to be at the same time talented enough to be good players and well-heeled enough to be able to afford to make the trip. These were days far removed from modern times when all manner of funding or fund-raising can be organised for a club or rep player travelling away.

So Eyton set out to interest prospective players and try to raise the money needed for backup. The return fare, by sea, to Great Britain at that time was £62. As well, £2000 had to be found for 'preliminary expenses'.

Surprisingly, Eyton did not have any problems in interesting the leading Maori players of the day. First, six or seven men came forward, then a few more, until there were over twenty. At that point the number of Maori players who wished to go petered out. Eyton wanted twenty-six tourists: with twenty-two he could not hope to do well.

But there were good ideas-men around in those far-off days too. And soon invitations were being offered not to Maori players but to leading Pakeha players who might, instead, look like Maori players!

And, sure enough, the invitations were accepted by four New Zealanders of European extraction and the team was born. They could not be called a New Zealand representative team as, quite simply, they were not. Soon, however, their nomenclature was confirmed: be they either Maori or Pakeha they were all New Zealand born, so they were dubbed the New Zealand Natives!

Now it's time to meet just some of the players who made up this pioneering band of intrepid travellers.

The Players

First, there were the Warbrick brothers, all five of them. Joe was the best known at the time and was actually the man whom Tom Eyton had contacted first on his return to New Zealand to look for the talent to tour. With Joe, from within the Warbrick family, were William, Fred, Arthur and Alf, all accomplished players.

Then there were the three Wynyard brothers, who all had colourful nicknames. One was 'Tab', and the other two were known as 'Pie' and 'Sherry'.

There were two players who were later to represent New Zealand. They were the Poneke boys from Wellington, Davey Gage and Tom Ellison. Also in the team was E. Ihimaira who became known and instantly recognisable as

'Smiler'. And there was Dick Taiaroa, one of the last surviving chiefs of the Ngai Tahu tribe.

The four Pakehas in the team were Bill 'Mother' Elliott (who was to be the last survivor of the team, living on well into the 1950s), Paddy Keogh, C. 'Barlow' Madigan and G. A. 'Bully' Williams.

The Build-up

The team of Natives assembled in Napier, Joe Warbrick's home town at the time, and on 23 June 1888 they played their first game together. They beat Hawke's Bay by 5 points to nil. For the New Zealand part of the trip tries were to count for 1 point, conversions 2 points and dropped goals and goals from marks counted for 3 points.

Other matches in New Zealand followed and after a month of solid travel, mostly by rail, the team had built up the reasonably satisfying record of having had 6 wins and 1 loss. It was against Otago in game eight that the first documented outside opinion on the playing merits of the Native team was given. An Otago official, perhaps

Previous page
Pictures of the fabulous Native team of 1888–9 are rare. Here is one taken just before the playing of one of their 107 tour fixtures, spread over fourteen months! You can see that they strongly represent what later All Black rugby teams came to look like. Yet the Natives were far from being New Zealand representatives. Their jerseys were black and originally adorned with a gold leaf, similar to Canada's maple leaf. At the insistence of the English a more unmistakable New Zealand emblem was sewn on. Thus, New Zealand sports teams began to play with the fernleaf emblem.

reflecting a general opinion prevailing that the tour would be a flop, wrote to an English official and said he did not believe the tourists would win a game. A similar sentiment was then echoed in one English paper when a writer claimed that the Natives were only fit to play against English schoolboy teams. Incidentally, to bolster the Otago man's pessimism, Otago beat the Natives by 8–0; but the Natives reversed the outcome by 1–0 in a second game.

So the team had played nine matches together when they sailed from New Zealand. By this stage the first of the many injuries the team would have had struck: Joe Warbrick had been crocked with a leg worry and was little or no use for the rest of the tour. And remember, I am talking here of a tour that was to last over fourteen months!

Boiler Room Training Sessions

At the first port of call, Melbourne, the Natives found there was little or no rugby football played in the manner to which they were accustomed, so they simply adapted to the local customs and played the home team using the Australian Rules Football format. Again, one could never imagine teams of today simply changing their rules to meet with the demands of the locals.

After a week in Australia the Natives again boarded their ship and sailed for Great Britain. To keep fit in the cramped conditions on board, the players each did time working in the ship's boiler room.

It was a long trip to the 'Old Country' and as a result the team did not play from 15 August 1888 until 3 October in the same year.

By then the team had been welcomed in England and to their surprise there was initial disappointment from the locals that (a) the team were not all Maori and (b) those in the team who were Maori did not always look the image of what English people expected Maori should look like (i.e., not dark enough!) and (c) there was general disappointment that the Natives did not run around doing war dances all the time and wear rings in their noses!

In his book *Rugby Football, Past and Present,* which was published in 1896, Tom Eyton wrote of the many problems the team faced on their arrival in England. One of the main ones was, of course, money. Eyton was seemingly obsessed with the financial success of the venture and there were many references in the book's text to how the crowd attendance figures fluctuated for each game.

Matches Galore

When the tour started in Great Britain in October 1888 the team were confirmed to play only a standard number of tour games, maybe twenty or so. But the immediate public curiosity in them led to more games being arranged as the party journeyed along. Soon the Natives were caught up in a whirlwind of matches, all over the country and at such frequent intervals that recovery time was well-nigh impossible.

The team won its first three games, spread over a week, which is a standard duration even in modern times. Then word got out about this crazy band of blackshirted New Zealanders who could play the sport of rugby in a winning way and other offers came flooding in to Thomas Eyton and his assistant manager, James Scott.

Soon the team was every playing other day. Between 20 and 31 October they had five games. Then, as the total of fixtures played built up, they found themselves on a veritable merry-go-round from which there was no leaping off. In November there was one spell where six games were played in eight days (with only one loss, incidentally) and at Christmas-time there were eight games in sixteen days.

But if the tough schedule of games ever bothered the Native team they never seemed to worry. Soon the tour became a series of adventures that, surely, no men of a sporting nature before or since could have matched.

In the first tour game Eyton wrote, 'The attendance was good for an off day. The Native team appeared in their Maori mats and gave their war cry — Ake Ake Kia Kaha!' Then, against Carlisle: 'Those of our team who elected to play in this match were quite dismayed by the weather. We begged Mr Scott to postpone the match for another day . . . but our boys were thus driven to the ground in a storm of sleet. When the second spell of the game commenced it was so cold that three of the Carlisle players were too stiff with cold to continue. Our fellow, Keogh, also had to remain under shelter. The game became a farce. We scored whenever we liked and it was so wet that some of our backs stood about with raincoats thrown over their shoulders'. And another example: 'Against Oxford University, some waggish undergraduates decided that seeing our team was from down underneath their world the names of the Native players should be published in the programme in an upside down manner!' Quotes like that will serve to tell you that this tour became a classic and yet it is fully deserving of being part of this book. Its bizarre nature and colourful stories of the unusual happenings make it one of the most memorable yet underrated New Zealand sports stories.

In the end the Natives of 1888 passed into the New Year having played thirty-six matches in Great Britain for twenty-two wins, eleven losses and three draws. As the team limped into January (for by now the injury toll was hindering many of the players' physical capabilities) they did not know, I am sure, that their tour still had eight months and over fifty games to go!

By now many of the team were becoming big favourites with the crowds who passed stories of their feats from village to village as the tour progressed. They spoke of Davey Gage, who was nicknamed 'Pony' or 'Iron Man' because of the incredible number of matches he pulled himself together for. Day after day Gage would pull on his playing gear and face fresh tacklers and 'hackers' (the word that described the manner in which players could be hacked with the feet during play. Perfectly legal then but not now). Gage never seemed to be hurt though there were those who said he died in 1916 never truly having recovered from the rigours of playing so hard so often without respite. Then there was Dick Taiaroa, who often waved to the crowd as he played and who one day blew a kiss to the opposition fullback as he ran round him on his way to another

try. Sadly for Taiaroa, but great for the humour of that particular story, is the reminder of the crowd's cheer as the fullback recovered to chase and catch the flying New Zealander.

Classic Stories

And talking of humour, how about Paddy Keogh ('Pakeha Paddy' they called him) scoring on one occasion by tricking the other team well and truly. Instead of running with the ball tucked under his arm as is the convention, he made one run with the ball pushed firmly up under his jumper. He called out, 'Who's got it?, Who's got it?', and then ran past the defensive line to produce the leather again and score a try.

And there were other classic stories of humour and incident as well:

Take the day they played Middlesex. The ground chosen for the game was on Lord Sheffield's estate and it was a private game with only the very best of Lord Sheffield's landed gentry friends invited to attend. As host, the estate owner decided to turn the day into a social occasion and a sumptuous luncheon was laid out. The Natives arrived and fell upon the food as though they had not eaten for weeks (though actually there was never a word from any of them about being poorly fed). Soon the rustic band of New Zealanders, many of whom had never seen a spread like this before their eyes, were as they used to say in those days — 'pickled' from all the overeating and, dare one say it of rugby players, overdrinking! Soon the good Lord (Sheffield, I mean) offered the team a photograph of themselves in the splendid surroundings. Alas for his noble intentions, not all of the Natives could be found. Though it was only moments before the kickoff a number of them were noticed to be absent and, sure enough, those that were missing were soon found sleeping it off under some tree or hedge.

The good Lord Sheffield further hammered home the advantages of his lifestyle by sending out servants at half-time with more champagne and grapes served on silver platters. The record book shows that the Natives lost that match by 0–9!

At another match the prevailing feeling among the locals that these South Seas islanders did not look enough like wild men led the New Zealanders to produce a publicity stunt. On their arrival at the next town's railway station they leapt from the train complete with white paint, black face masks and carrying amateurish-looking spears. They made blood-curdling cries and yells and from all accounts they thoroughly impressed the locals who then, one presumes, felt inclined to turn up and watch these wild men play!

In fact, gazing upon the Maori players was a favourite pastime of many a curious British person. They were particularly fascinated with the stocky build of the New Zealanders. One man in the team faced so many questions about the size of his calf muscles and eventually grew so tired of all the enquiries he cut off one leg of his trousers so that the limb that was causing all the fascination could be permanently in view!

In fact, if the snippets of research material that are available are anything to go by, the Native rugby team

of 1888–89 broke a few hearts on their tour. One of the players, the one they called 'Smiler', was presented with a ring by a Iady of supposedly very high social standing. 'Smiler' wrote home with pride that the ring must have cost all of six pounds!

But the affection from the players for the people of England, Ireland, and Wales was nothing compared to the bond of devotion that the merry band of New Zealanders were building up among themselves. At nights they would sit with their arms around each others' shoulders and sing of home, so far away. They also would produce a regular and improving version of their team song 'On the Ball' for their own pleasure as well as that of their hosts. The song, written by a New Zealander, became a big hit all over Great Britain.

And so the epic narrative of this story wound on around all of England, Ireland and Wales as the tour continued to unfold for the players of the New Zealand Native Football Team. It was New Year 1889 and the tour was still far from over. Almost every day they would climb on board a modest third-class train and take their seats in their private carriage (hired for the tour for a cost of £400) to journey to the next game. On board they would maybe begin a card game of 'penny nap' to pass the time or sit mending their threadbare playing equipment. On several days the team actually played their game in their street clothes as they could not always afford to pay their laundry bills. It was either that or the tight schedule of fixtures meant that their only set of playing gear was hanging out to dry in some other place! For some players, like Davey Gage, every new game meant putting on his playing gear yet again. Gage was incredible: he was always fit to take up the football battle. He fully merited and lived up to the name 'Iron Man'.

No Complaints

In January a further thirteen games were undertaken, then eleven more in February and finally fourteen more matches in the month of March. The strain of physically being up and running must have been enormous for the Natives, but they struggled on. Some days they could not field a full squad of fifteen players, so heavy was the toll of injuries. For most of their games in the United Kingdom the team was chosen from twenty-three fit players. But, when Mr Eyton's precious financial position was deemed too precarious, only fifteen players were allowed to travel from the team's hotel base of that particular time to the game of the day. But again, one has to say, there is little or no documentation of any complaints by the players at the tough and extremely rigorous tour schedule.

Included in the team's itinerary were full internationals against three of the home nations; Ireland were turned back by 13–4 but Wales beat the tourists by 5–0 and England beat them as well, by 7–0. For some reason, which remains obscure, the Natives did not play in Scotland.

In the end, of course, it all had to end. On 27 March 1889 the Natives played and beat Southern Counties at Leyton by 3–1, a game that was to be the last of their tour of Great Britain. In fact it was their seventy-fourth

game of rugby since arriving six months earlier! Their wins did not quite reach fifty (in fact they won forty-nine times) but they only lost twenty times and had five draws. It was a fantastic effort by the team who, in the end, developed a tremendous rapport and confidence in themselves. Davey Gage was a vital part of the team's play as he appeared in sixty-eight of the games played in Great Britain.

But if, on their departure for home, Gage and the other players thought that their tour was over, there were other plans in the minds of Tom Eyton, James Scott and Joe Warbrick.

They knew that the team would be stopping off in Australia again on the way home, so yet more fixtures were arranged for the weary wanderers to play.

There was even a game played in Egypt, though it must have been so rough and rustic it does not appear in the official team records. According to the stories, the team's ship had to wait in the Suez Canal for another to pass so the players disembarked briefly and played a game on the sandy soil of Egypt. That appearance by New Zealand rugby players in Egypt became a forerunner of many games of rugby that were played in that country by New Zealand servicemen in the Second World War.

Back in Australia, the Natives again played a game with the strange rules of that country, against the Melbourne Rugby Football Club, with whom they had been in opposition nine months before. The locals were reported to be astonished at the keenness of the touring band of New Zealanders. Apparently the good keen Kiwis (one must presume they were called that then!) used to practise at night using the moon as their illumination.

Then it was on up to Sydney for another half-dozen matches, then a couple of games in each of Brisbane, Toowoomba and Ipswich before the team set sail, homeward bound at last, for New Zealand.

Even though they must have been very tired the Natives went unbeaten in Australia, although again the team was in the news a lot. In several of their games they met opposition teams who were allowed to field up to eighteen men and there was a scandal of sorts when, in the final game, it was alleged that four of the New Zealanders had been influenced as to how to play their game by several of the local bookmakers.

The 'tip' that some of the visiting team were not playing fairly prompted officialdom to step in and ask those concerned, at half time, whether it was so. When the players admitted that in fact they had been 'got at' by the bookmakers they were allowed to play on. The players involved must have feared that their honour was at stake as they all played brilliantly in the latter half of the game and on their return to New Zealand no further action was taken.

After the game, one of the Queensland players said that the 'Maoris' (for that was their common nickname all over the world) had played so well that 'we only saw the ball at put-ins, and we never saw it again!'

Home at Last

On their return home the team arrived in Bluff and played first in Invercargill to begin a farewell tour of the same country that had ridiculed their chances of success almost twelve months before. They immediately made their presence felt in New Zealand by taking the field against Southland with only fourteen men. (There were some injuries but their playing numbers were reduced mainly because the four who had transgressed the law, with the aid of the bookmakers, were still under suspension). After another injury they finished the match with only thirteen on the field! Of course, they won the game.

The canny Southlanders then promptly negotiated a sixteen-man opposing team for next day in Gore but the Natives thrashed them anyway by 16–3.

One wonders what the Otago official who made the widely reported comment to his English friend about the weakness of the Natives must have felt when they returned to Dunedin two days after that to beat the Otago team by 11–8.

The Native team played their final match, anywhere in the world, in Auckland on 24 August 1889. That they lost was hardly surprising as the game was actually the 107th they had had on their momentous circumnavigation of the globe. At the end of the game it is reported that many of the team were absolutely dog-tired and exhausted. One of them, Wi Karauria, had been getting progressively sicker as the tour had progressed and the strain eventually took its toll. The poor man died soon after the team came home. With him in his coffin at his burial was his precious and proudly worn Native Team cap which had also made the journey with him around the world. Indeed, today there are only four of those caps 'above ground' in assorted rugby museums. Those four belonged to the four European players. All the other caps that the players wore as a mark of recognition eventually went to rest with the six full-blooded and sixteen half-caste Maori team-mates.

Even though there was much of the pioneering spirit in what the Native team attempted, their tour had repercussions that lived long in the game of rugby union. The massive length of their effort was emulated by many teams in rugby in the decades that followed. Indeed, the Natives were considered to have set the style of the 'hard case' type of rugby tour that is still in evidence today — a tour where the rugby is serious and so is the social side! There was an underlying seriousness in Tom Eyton's idea that was borne out by the fact that the team's feats as rugby players are remembered even today — almost 100 years on — and so are the names of the leading men who took part. Among them are names like Eyton, Gage, Ellison, Wynyard, Warbrick, Keogh — and of course the always happy 'Smiler' Ihimaira.

The 1888–9 Natives were a team to be reckoned with as serious early ambassadors for the game, yet they are, because of the many unusual aspects of their tour, totally deserving of being included in any study of the strange and bizarre stories of New Zealand sports.